T0303890

ROUTLEDGE STUDIES ON THE

FINANCIAL SECTOR
OF THE
AMERICAN ECONOMY

edited by

STUART BRUCHEY
ALLAN NEVINS PROFESSOR EMERITUS
COLUMBIA UNIVERSITY

A ROUTLEDGE SERIES

INSTITUTIONAL SHAREHOLDER ACTIVISM

THE CHANGING FACE OF CORPORATE OWNERSHIP

MICHAEL J. RUBACH

Routledge
Taylor & Francis Group

NEW YORK AND LONDON

First published by Garland Publishing, Inc

This edition published 2011 by Routledge
711 Third Avenue, New York, NY 10017
2 Park Square, Milton Park, Abingdon, Oxon, OX14 4RN

Published in 1999 by
Garland Publishing, Inc.
A Member of the Taylor & Francis Group

Library of Congress Cataloging-in-Publication Data
Library of Congress Cataloging-in-Publication Data is available
from the Library of Congress.

Institutional shareholder activism: the changing face of coporate
ownership / by Michael J. Rubach

ISBN 0–8153–3502–4

Publisher's Note
The publisher has gone to great lengths to ensure the quality of this reprint
but points out that some imperfections in the original may be apparent.

To my wife, Patricia,
without whose love and support
this book would not have been written.

Contents

vii

Acknowledgments

The author would like to acknowledge the contributions of a number of individuals to the research and writing of this book. My dissertation committee chair, Dr. Terrence C. Sebora, whose help throughout my doctoral studies made the process both educational and endurable; Professors Lester A. Digman, Metropolitan Federal Bank Professor of Management, Thomas S. Zorn, Rachel Parham Carveth Professor of Finance, and Steven L. Willborn, Cline Williams Professor of Law, the other members of my dissertation committee at the University of Nebraska at Lincoln, whose comments and suggestions were invaluable in directing the research; P. A. Vance and M. Barbara Rief, whose editorial suggestions enhanced the manuscript; and my secretaries, Karen Forey at the University of Nebraska at Omaha and Cathy Watson at the University of Nebraska at Lincoln, whose assistance throughout my doctoral program helped me complete the process, and ultimately, this book.

Figures and Tables

List of Abbreviations

CalPERS = California Public Employees Retirement System
CalSTRS = California State Teachers Retirement System
CII = Council of Institutional Investors
ColPERS = Colorado Public Employees Retirement System
DOL = US Department of Labor
ERISA = Employee Retirement and Income Security Act of 1974
FSBA = Florida State Board of Administration
IRRC = Investor Responsibility Research Center, Inc.
NYSCR = New York State Common Retirement System
PSERS = Pennsylvania Public Schools Employees Retirement System
SEC = US Securities and Exchange Commission
SWIB = State of Wisconsin Investment Board
TIAA-CREF = Teachers Insurance and Annuity Association–College Retirement Equities Fund
US = United States of America

INSTITUTIONAL
SHAREHOLDER
ACTIVISM

CHAPTER 1

Introduction

This book examines the shareholder activism of institutional investors and the effect of shareholder activism on portfolio performance. Institutional shareholder activism includes both traditional mechanisms of influence (e.g., filing shareholder proposals) and relationship investing (e.g., long-term interorganizational contacts between owners and a corporation's top managers).[1] Institutional investors/owners include private and public pension funds, mutual funds, bank trusts, insurance companies, endowments, and foundations. This book is unique in addressing the shareholder activism of a large sample of institutional owners: 118 institutions headquartered in the US.

The interrelationships among the major participants in corporate governance—owners, boards of directors, and top management teams—affect corporate decision making and, ultimately, firm performance. This book investigates the implications of changes in corporate ownership structure caused by the increasing presence of institutional investors and the effects of these ownership changes on how institutional investors manage their portfolios. New patterns of ownership by institutional investors are challenging the traditional paradigm of corporate governance. Understanding the role of institutional owners in the governance picture has importance for theory building, practice, and regulation.

This book, like much of the previous research, often discusses institutional owners as though they are homogeneous or a monolithic group. While often referred to, spoken of, or depicted as homogenous, institutional shareholders are quite heterogeneous, and their owners or beneficiaries, economic motivations, and political contexts differ substantially.

Moreover, they function under different legal and regulatory constraints. These differences lead institutions to use the power of share ownership to pursue different philosophies and actions. Some institutions appear to follow a passive governance policy, while others seem to have adopted a more "hands on" position.

Agency theory would indicate that the shareholders of a firm should be the monitors of its operators, its board of directors and top management team. However, there are numerous economic and legal constraints which are disincentives to monitoring. Despite these disincentives, some institutional shareholders continue to act in ways which monitor or constrain companies' operations. This book examines why institutions are shareholder activists and what is the effect of this activism on corporate operations, structures, and performance. Agency theory has been the predominate paradigm for studying corporate governance structures. However, agency theory provides an incomplete picture.[2] Constituency theory[3] and stewardship theory, which both presume a firm's management seeks to maximize total organizational performance, have been advanced as alternative frameworks.[4] This book attempts to add to a better understanding of the position and role of institutional shareholders in US corporate governance by viewing constituency theory and stewardship theory as complements to agency theory.

Recognizing the potential power of institutions to influence corporate decisions, this book seeks to answer four questions: (1) Are institutional owners actively involved in the strategic affairs of companies in their portfolios? (2) Which forms of activism do institutional owners employ (confrontational mechanisms, such as filing shareholder proposals, or relationship building mechanisms)? (3) Which forms of activism employed are most effective? and (4) Does the type of institution affect its pursuit of shareholder activism?

There are claims that the new patterns of decision making, which institutional ownership is creating, will result in enhanced corporate performance.[5] It is argued that shareholder activism has, and will continue to have, a significant impact on corporate governance structures and processes and on firm leadership.[6] To the contrary, others suggest that the new ownership structures and the concomitant shareholder activism may, indeed, be the wrong sort of managerial discipline altogether and actually may decrease firm value.[7] This split of opinion suggests that empirical research is necessary to determine if shareholder activism truly improves firm performance. This book seeks to add to the research in this area.

Contrary to what prior reports of the activities by a small number of institutional owners may intimate, the results from data gathered from a sample of 118 institutional owners suggest that most institutions follow a passive policy; only about 10% report the practice of confrontational activism or relationship investing with boards; some institutions (about 30%) actively attempt to influence firms by establishing relationships with top managers; activism does not benefit their portfolios (shareholder activism does not improve corporate performance); the portfolio returns of institutions that report attempts to influence are lower than those that report making no such attempts; and activism is not related to specific institutional types or investment philosophies (e.g., maximizing financial returns only or maximizing financial and other returns).

Further, most responding institutional owners (over 54%) hire external fund managers. This creates a situation of "agents watching agents watching agents" which suggests that fund management may be a significant determinant of institutional activism. This finding intimates that future research should be aimed at studying the relationships between fund managers/money managers and their principals.

In terms of practical applications, the research has importance for institutional owners and their portfolios managers. In its attempts to determine the efficacy of the various shareholder activism mechanisms, it can provide institutions with empirical support for determining the effectiveness of pursuing various monitoring activities, including relationship investing and interorganizational relations. Indirectly, the results should aid corporate managers in their decision-making. Corporations will continue to be confronted with the growing presence of institutional shareholders. Strategically, in attempting to determine which activist mechanisms have been most effective in terms of firm performance, corporate managers may gain insight into which programs and structures are most beneficial to the corporation and its shareholders.

Finally, prior research has identified that governance systems are not necessarily inevitable results of trade and commerce, but are creatures of politics.[8] Regulations constrain the activities of institutional owners and the effectiveness of their activism. Some commentators have complained that these regulations have effectively prevented institutional owners from even pursuing activism.[9] Others have criticized the movement toward shareholder activism as an area ripe for meddling by inexperienced investors and for private gains which are achieved at the expense of the public.[10] This research investigated the efficacy of the present regulatory system. The findings provide evidence which supports the continuance of the present regulatory schema which permits institutional owners to monitor and regulate governance structures through private arrangements, not public regulation.

OUTLINE OF THE BOOK

The remainder of this book is organized into seven chapters. In Chapter 2, the author presents two conflicting views of US corporate governance: the traditional economic model (agency theory) versus the constituency model. An underlying assumption of the research is that there is a separation of ownership from control which creates agency costs.

Chapter 3 describes institutional heterogeneity. The argument is made that institutional owners/investors are not a homogeneous group as has often been depicted in prior writings and research. This book argues that institutional heterogeneity is a factor in the pursuit of shareholder activism.

Chapter 4 surveys the literature on institutional shareholder activism and its effects on corporate performance. The prior literature usually addresses the impact of activism on specific firm's performance. Few studies address the impact on portfolio performance. Also, most prior research has also centered upon the activities of a few large public pension plans, such as CalPERS. These large public pension plans have been the most vocal in their pursuit of activism, and have been the most studied because their records are accessible. This book differs from previous research by studying the activism of a broader range of institutional investors and institutional shareholder activism.

Chapter 5 describes the research model, identifies institutional owners and the top managers of the corporations. Institutional shareholder activism is defined, and the definition differs from many prior studies because it includes relationship investing as a mechanism of shareholder activism. Four research questions and eight hypotheses are presented. The hypotheses address the four research questions and deal with the extent of shareholder activism, the investment philosophies of institutional owners, the effects of institutional shareholder activism on portfolio performance, and whether the type of institution affects any of these issues.

Chapter 6 describes the methodology of the research. The research is exploratory in nature trying to develop and test the extent of institutional shareholder activism, its determinants, and its effects on portfolio performance. No prior research has attempted to study institutional shareholder activism on a broad scale across institutional types. The independent and dependent variables used in the analysis are defined. The procedures used to collect the data and how that data was analyzed are described. The chapter concludes by discussing the statistical tests used to analyze the data and the appropriateness of these tests.

Chapter 7 presents and analyzes the results. The limitations of the research methodology and the results are identified.

Chapter 8 discusses the implications for institutional owners with respect to the pursuit of activism, for corporate managers with respect to which institutions are activists, and for regulators with respect to the scope of activism. Also, the chapter identifies areas for future research.

NOTES

[1] "Relationship investing" is a cooperative association between an organization's owners and management. It envisions a long-term advisory relationship with its essence being communication among the parties. This concept is often referred to as "relational investing." Ian Ayers and Peter Cramton, "Relational Investing and Agency Theory," *Cardozo Law Review* 15 (1994): 1033-1066. There is some confusion concerning what relational investing encompasses. This is especially true in the finance literature. Therefore, the term "relationship investing" will be used herein.

[2] Gerald F. Davis and Tracy A. Thompson, "A Social Movement Perspective on Corporate Control," *Administrative Science Quarterly* 39 (1994): 141-173.

[3] This book uses the term "constituency theory" to describe a school of corporate governance which views the corporation as a system of stakeholders within a larger social system. The use of the term "stakeholder" is avoided in order to avoid confusing constituency theory with general stakeholder theories espoused in corporate ethics and social responsibility debates. Under corporate governance constituency or stakeholder theory, the purpose of the firm is to create wealth or value for all of its constituents or stakeholders. Margaret M. Blair, *Ownership and Control: Rethinking Corporate Governance for the Twenty-first Century*, (Washington, D.C.: The Brookings Institution, 1995), 332. The theory advocates that constituents or stakeholders should have a voice in corporate decision making, creating alliances between critical constituents and top managers. Michael E. Porter, *Capital Choices: Changing the Way America Invests in Industry*, (Washington, D.C.: Research report presented by the Council on Competitiveness and cosponsored by the Harvard Business School, 1992). Jeffrey S. Harrison and Caron H. St. John, "Managing and Partnering with External Stakeholders," *Academy of Management Executive* 10, no. 2 (1996): 46-60.

[4] For a brief discussion of constituency or stakeholder theory see Shaun Turnbull, "Corporate Governance: Its Scope, Concerns and Theories," *Corporate Governance* 5, no 4 (1997): 180-205. For discussions of stewardship theory, see

James H. Davis, F. David Schoorman, and Lex Donaldson, "Towards a Steward-ship Theory of Management," *Academy of Management Review* 22 (1997): 20–47; Lex Donaldson and J. H. Davis, "Stewardship Theory or Agency Theory: CEO Governance and Shareholder Returns," *Australian Journal of Management*, 16 (1991): 49-64. Mark A. Fox and Robert T. Hamilton, "Ownership and Diver-sification: Agency Theory or Stewardship Theory," *Journal of Management Stud-ies* 31, no. 1 (1994): 69-81.

[5] Jayne W. Barnard, "Institutional Investors and the New Corporate Gover-nance," *North Carolina Law Review* 69 (1991): 1135-1187.

[6] James P. Hawley, Andrew T. Williams, and John U. Miller, "Getting the Herd to Run: Shareholder Activism at the California Public Employees Retire-ment System (CalPERS)," *Business & the Contemporary World* 7, no. 4 (1994): 26-48.

[7] Roberta Romano, "Public Pension Fund Activism in Corporate Gover-nance Reconsidered," *Columbia Law Review* 94 (1993): 795-853. Edward B. Rock, "The Logic and (Uncertain) Significance of Institutional Shareholder Ac-tivism," *The Georgetown Law Journal* 79 (1991): 445-506.

[8] Mark J. Roe, *Strong Managers, Weak Owners: The Political Roots of American Corporate Finance*, (Princeton, NJ: Princeton University Press, 1994).

[9] Ibid. Bernard S. Black, "The Value of Institutional Investor Monitoring: The Empirical Evidence," *UCLA Law Review* 39 (1992): 895-939. John C. Cof-fee, Jr., "The SEC and the Institutional Investor: A Half-Time Report," *Cardozo Law Review* 15 (1994): 837-907.

[10] Rock, "The Logic and (Uncertain) Significance of Institutional Share-holder Activism." Catherine M. Daily, Jonathon L. Johnson, Alan E. Ellstrand, and Dan R. Dalton, *Institutional Investor Activism: Follow the Leaders?* (paper presented at annual meeting of the Academy of Management, Boston, Massachu-setts, 9-14 August 1996).

CHAPTER 2

Institutional Ownership and Corporate Governance

AT&T's payment of a $5.2 million bonus to its CEO in a year the company barely breaks even is publicly criticized; the composition and structure of the boards of directors of Disney and Archer-Daniels-Midland are under attack; and K-Mart's and Woolworth's business strategies are questioned following poor earnings performances. In each of these instances, the attacks and pressures to change are coming from a source not previously perceived as a participant in corporate strategy and policy matters: the institutional owner. Fundamentally, where and how an organization operates and how its performance is measured are responsive to the will of its owners. The increasing presence of institutional owners is altering the ownership structure of firms, which may alter corporate strategies and policies. As ownership changes, how, where, and why firms compete may also change.[11]

Corporate governance investigates the internal functioning of business corporations and how corporate strategies are determined. The central issues of corporate governance involve who controls the corporation, who makes the critical strategic decisions, who is responsible for those decisions, and who has claims against the revenues and assets of the firm.[12] An organization's ownership structure, a major element of its corporate governance, often determines whether the firm is successful.

Berle and Means were the foremost, if not the first, commentators to identify the corporate governance paradigm that recognizes a separation of ownership from control.[13] The Berle-Means paradigm is often referred to as "managerialism" and the period of its ascendancy is dubbed the "managerial era."[14] In this paradigm, shareholders, although the owners of the corporation, typically do not control policy making or strategic decision making within the corporation. The management team is recognized as the group which controls corporate decision making. The shareholders, due to their dispersed ownership, have little power to influence corporate policies. While recognized as providers of capital and the claimants of the residual returns or rents of the corporation, shareholders are inevitably cast in the role of passive owners. They are expected to refrain from interfering in the ongoing operations of companies. If a shareholder does not like the way a firm is run, then the shareholder is expected to do "the Wall Street Walk"—sell her shares and get out.

Since Berle and Mean's 1929 study, the landscape of corporate governance in the United States (US) has undergone a tremendous change. Institutional owners have become major players in governance structures due to their increased ownership and share concentrations. Institutional owners generally include private pension funds, public pension funds, mutual funds, banks, insurance companies, nonbank trusts, endowments, and foundations.[15]

The sheer number of institutional investors has grown dramatically. Table 2.1 shows the increases from 1985 to 1990 in number of institutions which owned stock in the 25 largest US corporations.

Table 2.1 Numbers of Institutional Owners (1985 and 1990)

The number of institutional owners which filed SEC disclosure forms (Form 13F) and which held stock in the 25 largest US corporations[16]

	Number of Institutional Owners	Average Number of Institutional Owners Per Company
1985	8,779	351
1990	13,234	531

The number of equities owned by institutional investors, as a percentage of all US publicly traded equities has also grown substantially. Figure 2.1 traces the growth of institutional investor equity ownership from 1955 to 1990. The collective ownership of institutional owners has risen from 23% in 1955 to 53.3% in 1990.[17] Increases in the number of institutional owners and in the percentage ownership of US publicly traded equities by institutions have been linked to the increased popularity of mutual funds as investment vehicles and the increased creation and funding of pension plans.[18] By the year 2000, it is estimated that institutional investors will hold over two-thirds of the equity capital of all US businesses, and within this group of institutions, pension plans (private and public) will be the fastest growing sector.[19] If all, or any part of, the social security system is privatized, the extent of institutional ownership will likely be even greater.

Figure 2.1 Percentage Ownership by Institutional Owners of U.S. Publicly Traded Equities

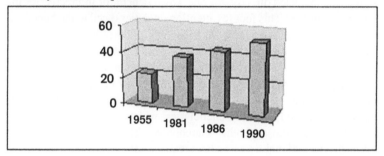

A consequence of the increase in institutional investor presence is the emergence of concentrated corporate ownership and changes in the concepts of ownership and control. The new institutional ownership is transforming the power structures and relationships within corporations. The prior paradigm, Berle-Means, of the publicly traded corporation with widely dispersed individual investors who are passive may no longer be accurate.

OWNERSHIP

Ownership is an elusive concept. It is generally understood to be a bundle of rights that includes: (1) the right to possess and use a property, (2) the right to the rents derived from the property, (3) the right to control its use, and (4) the right to transfer all or part of the property to others. Ownership, as it relates to corporations and shareholding, is problematic. Shareholders, unlike other owners, do not have a right to possess, use, or transfer corporate assets. Shareholders' rights are embodied in share ownership, i.e., the rights of ownership of a separate entity. Shareholders' ownership rights are limited, generally comprise only a part of the bundle, and are residual, i.e., shareholders are entitled to whatever remains after all revenues are collected and all debts, expenses, and contractual obligations are paid.[20]

Under the Berle-Means paradigm, shareholders as financial capital providers are recognized as residual claimants. There is a growing debate, however, over whether shareholders are the only residual claimants, or even the primary residual claimants. Others may lay claim to parts of the firm's residual rents, diminishing the rights of owners and investors. Employees and society are recognized as additional capital providers who may have equal claims to residual rents.[21]

The concept of residual ownership rights implicitly recognizes that rights can be owned directly, for one's own benefit, or indirectly, for the benefit of another. This focuses attention on duties owed to the beneficial owners and unearths a myriad of accountability problems. Institutional owners are generally indirect owners: they hold and invest other peoples' monies. The beneficiaries of institutions are often among the alternate claimants to a firm's rents. This is especially true for employees, the beneficiaries of pension plans. Thus, institutional owners may have policy agendas fashioned by their beneficiaries, which differ from the classic model and from those of other shareholders. The indirect ownership of stock by institutional owners also creates a dilemma. The institutional owners are really agents for their owners or beneficiaries,[22] which creates an additional set of duties and accountabilities and further muddles the relationships between owners and the firm's managers. [23]

Shareholder rights usually center on the residual right to control the company and the right to transfer the property; each right is defined and limited by an evolving legal process. The right to residual control is the right to make decisions as to the use of an asset. Under the Berle-Means paradigm, shareholders lost the power to effectively control corporate policies and decision making. However, the increased presence of institutions is rekindling the ownership right to residual control. The increased concentration of stock ownership by institutions is creating a source of power for these shareholders.[24] There is some evidence that institutions, as concentrated owners, are beginning to wield this power by influencing firm policies, participating in firm decision making, and exercising their voting rights to control managers' actions. At a minimum, the power of institutions may be the equivalent of a veto power over all major financial transactions of the corporations which they own.[25] The unusual bundling of ownership rights within a corporation complicates the relationships among shareholders, directors, and managers, and alters the corporate governance structure.

Conflicting Views of Corporate Governance

Clearly, the growing presence of institutional ownership of major corporations is changing how corporations are viewed. Prior theories no longer adequately explain the motivations of institutions, and the empirical research in the area of institutional activism is inconclusive.

Hill and Snell provide a research model for corporate governance (see Figure 2.2) which includes the constructs of ownership structure, strategy, and firm performance.[26] They hypothesized that strategies would differ among firms with different stockholder concentrations, ultimately influencing firm performance.

Figure 2.2 The Corporate Governance Model

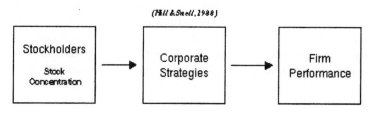

Most of the empirical research with regard to institutional owners and institutional shareholder activism has focused upon the performance dimension, assuming corporate value is a function of the structure of equity ownership. The research generally looks at firm performance in financial terms.[27] The actual relationship between institutional ownership and firm performance, however, is still a relatively unexplored area. Ownership structure implicitly influences whether the owners pursue activism or passivity (i.e., whether the owners will become involved in sculpting the strategies of the firm, specifically influencing where, how, and why firms compete). The actions of the owners, depending upon their activism, are aimed at different parties. Finally, the model addresses the issue of whether the activities, or non-activities, have a positive or negative effect on firm performance.

As mentioned earlier, ownership of public corporations is changing, and institutions have become the principal owners of firms. The changing roles of institutional owners and their exhibited power is not a new phenomenon. In 1965, Baum and Stiles identified the emerging ability of institutional investors to shift the balance of power from managers. Their argument, while not as fine grained as contemporary writings, is similar:

> Institutional investors possess power in their portfolio corporations....
> this power, exercised or nonexercised, serves as a sanction or endorsement of management....[28]

Despite many disincentives which constrain collective action and monitoring, over the last decade institutional owners have led a movement of shareholder activism to both monitor and change US corporate governance. The new shareholder activism is often an activism of cooperative, not antagonistic, relationships and raises issues which may not be best explained by assessing whether institutional owners are effective monitors.[29]

The study of corporate governance is not strictly about transactions and economics; it addresses the fundamental relationships among owners, directors, and managers. The real issue no longer seems to be the separation of ownership and control or managerialism, but the activity or passivity of this new class of controlling shareholders.[30] Consequently, agency theory, with its focus on managerialism and shareholder-board-manager relationships and the costs to monitor these relationships may be too narrowly focused. Measures other than stock values may be necessary. So other theories such as constituency theory or stewardship theory may help explain the principal-agent relationship. Constituency theory and stewardship theory suggest that the participants enter into cooperative relationships where total firm wealth is maximized, not just the wealth of the principals (the shareholders). The relationships among boards, managers, and institutional owners and the roles of each in corporate governance may be better understood by discerning the differences and complements among agency theory, constituency theory and stewardship theory.[31]

THE MANAGERIAL VIEW

The managerial view of corporate governance or managerialism has its basis in the liberal-utilitarian model of classical economics. The model is also termed the simple finance model or agency model.[32] The consequences of the separation are generally referred to as agency costs, and agency theory has been the predominant paradigm for understanding and explaining corporate governance issues.[33] The modern large or public corporation and corporate governance scholarship, at least in the US, is still characterized by the principle of the separation of ownership and control.[34] While it is debatable what has caused this separation,[35] the dispersed ownership of stock creates agency problems.

Central to managerialism is the proposition that governance (the rules and institutions which constrain agents' actions) affects corporate performance. Under managerialism, the firm is run to maximize the return for the shareholders, who are the bearers of residual risk, and good governance equates with shareholder wealth maximization.[36] The norm of shareholder wealth maximization creates a structure in which the top management team and the directors act as the agents for the shareholders and are ultimately held accountable to the corporation's shareholders.

Figure 2.3 The Managerial View of Corporate Governance
MANAGERIAL VIEW

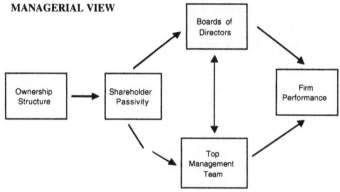

Figure 2.3 depicts the managerial view of corporate governance. Note the solid line and broken line leading from the shareholder passivity box. The solid line represents the power of shareholders to elect directors; the broken line depicts the indirect influence of shareholders over a corporation's top management team.

According to the managerial view, the world is populated by rational but self-interested maximizers who must be monitored and controlled.[37] This perspective assumes that management is prone to act in its own self-interest, rather than the principals' best interests. Therefore, someone or something must monitor and control these self-interested tendencies, and construct rules and incentives to effectively align the behaviors of managers (the agents) with the desires of the owners (the principals). Because equity holders bear the risk of the firm (and reap its profits), they are assumed to have the incentive to implement monitoring mechanisms or incentive devices to insure the alignment of the interests of the managers and directors with their own interests.[38] However, the corporate form and corporate governance have created considerable disincentives for shareholders to monitor managerial and board performance. The disincentives to collective action by dispersed shareholders are so considerable as to cast doubts on whether shareholders are even proper, let alone effective, monitors. The separation of ownership from control may make equity investors essentially powerless to influence corporate policies.

Managerialism further assumes that all shareholders are alike. It is implicit in the paradigm that institutions will play a minor role, occupying the same position as other public shareholders, divorced from management and without power to affect policy decision making. Also, all shareholders are assumed to be passive investors and will exit—sell their shares if they are dissatisfied with the performance of an investment.

THE CONSTITUENCY VIEW

The constituency view perceives the corporation as a social institution and emphasizes the social effects of corporate wealth creation. This perspective recognizes that corporate actions can have substantial public implications and that corporations can create wealth in more than one way. The theory recognizes that, while the capital investments of shareholders are a source of wealth, there are other sources, including the skills and knowledge of employees and the ability of the firm itself to utilize individual and firm knowledge.[39] This model views the world as populated by persons of limited rationality, who are embedded in a social context, a community. In this community, the principles of fairness and trust predominate.[40]

Figure 2.4 The Constituency View of Corporate Governance

CONSTITUENCY VIEW

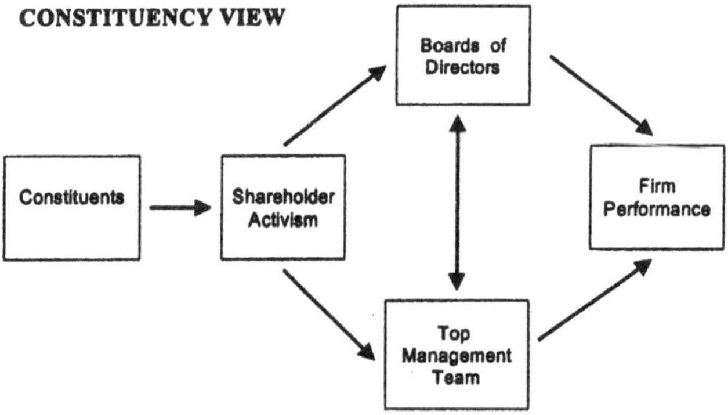

Figure 2.4 depicts the constituency view of corporate governance. Note the solid lines leading from the shareholder activism box. The solid lines represent the pursuit of relationship investing with boards of directors and the top management team. The constituency model posits that the

constituents or critical stakeholders of the organization will participate in organizational strategic decision-making, that they will not exit, but will exercise their voices.[41]

Perhaps partially reflecting a belief that ownership is not a meaningful concept as applied to modern public corporations or because shareholders do not have the exclusive and unfettered right to determine the destiny of the company,[42] the constituency perspective recognizes that firms owe duties to others besides shareholders. This is so even if a measure of residual risk is the key criterion used to evaluate for whom wealth should be generated. This view recognizes corporations as collective entities, with identities apart from the individuals who fill roles within them. Further, even within the separate groups of constituents not all members are viewed through the same lens or as equals. Under this perspective there is no prima facie priority of one set of interests and benefits over another. The job of the top management team is to maximize the total wealth creation of the firm. Pursuant to the constituency view, non-shareholders are recognized as bearers of residual risks, because they lose if the organization fails. The non-shareholder constituents (e.g., employees, suppliers, and customers) are recognized not only as necessary components in the decision making process, but as *participants* in the corporate governance structure.[43]

A different theory, which views managers not as self-interested opportunists but as individuals who want to do a good job and who act as caretakers or custodians of the firm's capitals, is stewardship theory.[44] Stewardship theory is based in the discipline of organizational behavior, not economics. Its goal is total wealth maximization with wealth and power being distributed among the various constituents of the firm. Implicitly, all constituents have roles, as coalitions and partnerships predominate. Institutional owners would exercise voice as active participants in the process.[45]

Historically, the advocacy of the constituency view is not new. In an immediate response to Berle and Mean's theory, Dodds took exception to the idea that corporations should be run for the sole benefit of shareholders. Dodds recognized corporations as entities with a social utility, implicitly acknowledging the rights of both society and employees. Dodds argued that:

> . . . the business corporation [is] an economic institution which has a social service as well as a profit-making function,... [and that] [b]usiness - which is the economic organization of society - is private property only in a qualified sense, and society may properly demand that it

be carried on in such a way as to safeguard the interests of those who deal with it either as employees or consumers even if the proprietary rights of its owners are thereby curtailed. [46]

The conflict between managerial and constituency theories is recognized in the heterogeneity of institutional owners and in the rationale for the practice of shareholder activism, which will be discussed in the next chapters.

NOTES

[11] Charles W. L. Hill and Scott A. Snell, "External Control, Corporate Strategy, and Firm Performance in Research-intensive Industries," *Strategic Management Journal* 9 (1988): 577-590.

[12] Blair, *Ownership and Control.* Margaret M. Blair, *Wealth Creation and Wealth Sharing: A Colloquium on Corporate Governance and Investments in Human Capital,* (Washington, D.C.: The Brookings Institute, 1996).

[13] Adolph A. Berle and Gardiner C. Means, *The Modern Corporation and Private Property* (New York: Macmillan, 1932).

[14] Davita S. Glasberg and Michael Schwartz, "Ownership and Control of Corporations," *Annual Review of Sociology* 9 (1983): 311-332. Alfred F. Conard, "Beyond Managerialism: Investor Capitalism," *Journal of Law Reform* 22, no. 1 (1988): 117-178. Samuel B. Graves and Sandra A. Waddock, "Institutional Ownership and Control: Implications for Long-term Corporate Strategy," *Academy of Management Executive* 4, no. 1 (1990): 75-83.

[15] James A Brickley, Ronald C. Lease, and Clifford W. Smith, Jr., "Ownership Structure and Voting on Antitakeover Amendments," *Journal of Financial Economics* 20 (1988): 267-291.

[16] The source of the data is Coffee, "The SEC and the Institutional Investor." Federal securities laws require institutions which exercise investment discretion and which hold securities that are traded on a national exchange or quoted on an automated quotation system to report their holding by filing Form 13F.

[17] William M. O'Barr and John M. Conley, *Fortune and Folly: The Wealth and Power of Institutional Investing,* (Homewood, IL: Business One Irwin, 1992).

[18] Stan Eakins, "An Empirical Investigation of Monitoring by Institutional Investors," *American Business Review* (January, 1995): 67-74.

[19] O'Barr and Conley, *Fortune and Folly.* Taken together, pension funds and mutual funds increased their share of equity ownership more than ten fold in forty years from 2.8% of total U.S. equities in 1950 to 38.1% in 1994. James P. Hawley and Andrew T. Williams, *Corporate Governance in the United States: The Rise of Fiduciary Capitalism: A Review of the Literature,"* [paper on-line] (Portland, Me.:

Lens, Inc., 1996); available from http://www.lens- inc.com/info/papers96/first/firstcontents.htm.

[20] Paul Milgrom and John Roberts, *Economics, Organization and Management*, (Englewood Cliffs, NJ: Prentice Hall, 1992)

[21] Eugene Schlossberger, "A New Model of Business: Dual-Investor Theory. *Business Ethics Quarterly* 4, no. 4 (1994): 459-474. Blair, *Ownership and Control.*

[22] Bernard S. Black, "Agents Watching Agents: The Promise of Institutional Investor Voice," *UCLA Law Review,* 39 (1992): 811-893.

[23] Hawley and Williams, "The Emergence of Fiduciary Capitalism."

[24] John Pound, "The Rise of the Political Model of Corporate Governance and Corporate Control," *New York University Law Review* 68 (1993): 1003-1071.

[25] Michael Useem, *Investor Capitalism: How Money Managers Are Changing the Face of Corporate America* (New York: Basic Books, 1996). O'Barr and Conley, Fortune and Folly.

[26] Hill and Snell, "External Control, Corporate Strategy, and Firm Performance."

[27] John J. McConnell and Henri Servaes, "Additional Evidence on Equity Ownership and Corporate Value," *Journal of Financial Economics* 27 (1990): 595-612. Harold Demsetz and Kenneth Lehn, "The Structure of Ownership: Causes and Consequences," *Journal of Political Economy* 93 (1985): 1155-1177. Randall Morck, Andrei Shleifer, and Robert W. Vishny, "Management Ownership and Market Valuation: An Empirical Analysis," *Journal of Financial Economics* 20 (1988): 293-315.

[28] Daniel J. Baum and Ned B. Stiles, *The Silent Partners: Institutional Investors and Corporate Control* (Syracuse, NY: Syracuse University Press, 1965), 65-66.

[29] Davis and Thompson, "A Social Movement Perspective."

[30] E. C. Lashbrooke, Jr., "The Divergence of Corporate Finance and Law in Corporate Governance," *South Carolina Law Review* 46 (1995): 449-469.

[31] There is debate over whether agency theory and stewardship theory are complementary or contradictory. Davis, Schoorman, and Donaldson in "Towards a Stewardship Theory of Management" contend that the theories are alternatives and not complements.

[32] Andrei Shleifer and Robert W. Vushny, "A Survey of Corporate Governance," *The Journal of Finance* 52, no. 2 (1997): 737-783. Turnbull, "Corporate Governance: Its Scope, Concerns and Theories."

[33] Michael C. Jensen and William H. Meckling, "Theory of the Firm: Managerial Behavior, Agency Costs and Ownership Structure," *Journal of Financial Economics* 3 (1976): 305-360.

[34] Stephen M. Bainbridge, "The Politics of Corporate Governance," *Harvard Journal of Law & Public Policy* 18, no. 3 (1995): 671-734.

[35] Roe, *Strong Managers, Weak Owners.*

[36] Harold Demsetz, "The Structure of Ownership and the Theory of the Firm," *Journal of Law and Economics* 26 (1983): 375-390. Armen A. Alchian and Harold Demsetz, "Production, Information Costs, and Economic Organization," *The American Economic Journal* 62 (1972): 777-795. James P. Hawley and Andrew T. Williams. "The Emergence of Fiduciary Capitalism." *Corporate Governance* 5, no. 4 (1997): 206-213.

[37] Eugene F. Fama and Michael C. Jensen, "Separation of Ownership and Control," *Journal of Law & Economics,* 26 (1983): 301-325.

[38] Jensen and Meckling, "Theory of the Firm." Ghosal and Moran raise the possibility that agency theory and its assumption of self interested opportunism is a self-fulfilling prophecy which necessitates further monitoring efforts on the part of principals and additional incentives to align agents' behavior. Sumantra Ghoshal and Peter Moran, "Bad for Practice: A Critique of the Transaction Cost Theory," *Academy of Management Review* 21 (1996): 21.

[39] Blair, *Ownership and Control.* Blair, *Wealth Creation and Wealth Sharing.*

[40] Lex Donaldson, "A Rational Basis for Criticisms of Organizational Economics: A Reply to Barney," *Academy of Management Review* 15, no. 3 (1990): 394-401. Lex Donaldson, "The Ethereal Hand: Organizational Economics and Management Theory," *Academy of Management Review* 15, no. 3 (1990): 369–381.

[41] Porter, *Capital Choices.* Hawley and Miller, "The Emergence of Fiduciary Capitalism."

[42] Martin Lipton, Theodore N. Mirvis, and Steven A. Rosenblum, "Corporate Governance in the Era of Institutional Ownership," *New York University Law Review* 70 (1995): 1145-1166. Bainbridge, "The Politics of Corporate Governance."

[43] Turnbull, "Corporate Governance: Its Scope, Concerns and Theories." Porter, *Capital Choices.* William R. Dill, "Public Participation in Corporate Planning: Strategic Management in a Kibitzer's World," *Long Range Planning* 8, no. 1 (1975): 57-63.

[44] Donaldson and Davis, "Stewardship Theory." Brian K. Boyd, "CEO Duality and Firm Performance: A Contingency Model," *Strategic Management Journal* 16 (1995): 301-312.

[45] Donaldson, "The Ethereal Hand."

[46] E. Merrick Dodds, Jr., "For Whom Are Corporate Managers Trustees?" *Harvard Law Review* 45, no. 7 (1932): 1148, 1162.

CHAPTER 3

Heterogeneity of Institutional Owners

Institutional owners are not a homogeneous group, but are quite heterogeneous. Their owners or beneficiaries, their economic and investment motivations, and their political contexts differ substantially. Moreover, institutions function under different legal, tax, and regulatory constraints.[47] O'Barr and Conley looked at the operation of institutional owners, and found that the institutions studied (three major state pension funds and six private pension funds) did differ, especially in terms of investment philosophy, the use of outside investment managers, portfolio techniques, such as the use of indexing, and their perceived roles in corporate governance. Useem and Sherman, Beldona and Joshi found similar differences in their studies of institutional investors.[48] Even within a single type of institutional investors (i.e., large public pension plans), there is the likelihood of heterogeneity.[49]

Much of the prior literature has assumed all institutional owners act alike. Only recently have researchers looked at the differences in the activities of institutions. Brickley, Lease and Smith present a classification or taxonomy which differentiates institutional investors based on whether the institutions and the businesses in which they invest (or have the potential to invest) have business relations other than the investment contracts. Such outside relationships permit the firm to influence the actions of an institutional investor, due to the institution's reliance on the business for future revenues. Institutional investors which rely upon the firm for business are characterized as pressure-sensitive; those which have no business relationships are classified as pressure-resistant.[50]

Banks, insurance companies, and nonbank trusts have been charac-

terized as pressure-sensitive organizations because they often rely upon
the firm for business. Public pension funds, mutual funds, and endowments and foundations have been categorized as pressure-resistant. Private pension plans, while not reliant upon a business for future revenues,
are characterized as pressure-sensitive because they are nominally controlled by the managements of the companies which establish them.
Also, private pension funds are likely to identify more with management.[51] Much of the effective activism is exhibited by large public pension funds. The pressure-sensitive institutions are not likely to be
activists.[52]

As indicated previously, institutional owners have generally included private pension plans, public pension plans, mutual funds, insurance companies, bank trusts, foundations, and endowments. The
differences among the various institutions are described below.

Private Pension Plans

Private pension funds are the largest category of institutional investors.
In 1994 they accounted for more than 17% of all equity ownership in the
US and their growth rate has been the fastest of any institutional group.
Their growth has been driven by a number of factors including favorable
tax treatment, the tax-free build-up of values, and the growth in the stock
market.[53]

Organizations establish private pension plans to provide compensation and retirement benefits for their employees. A federal statute,
ERISA, exclusively regulates private pension plans. ERISA provides
guidelines or standards for funding of the plans and for investing plan assets. There are general fiduciary duties to diversify a plan's portfolio
(e.g., the funds can not own more than 10% of the sponsoring company);
to exercise reasonable care in investing the assets; and to run the plan in
the best interests of the plan's participants and beneficiaries. The funds
contributed by the employer are tax deductible and income generated by
the funds is generally exempt from taxation, and the participants and
beneficiaries are only taxed upon their receipt of monies from the plans.
In defined benefit plans, if assets are insufficient to pay the plan's obligations, then the employer sponsor will likely be liable for the shortfall; the
employer, or in its place a governmental entity, the Pension Benefit
Guaranty Corporation, "insures" the payment of benefits. The same is
not true for defined contribution plans (e.g., 401(k) and profit sharing
plans) because the employer is generally not responsible for investment
losses, so long as the employer sponsor acted prudently in investing the

funds or in choosing outside fund managers. Private pension plans, which are often controlled by the companies which have created them, have not been identified with shareholder activism.[54] However, the Department of Labor, which administers ERISA, has issued regulations (commonly called the "Avon Letters") which can be interpreted to require monitoring by institutional owners as part of the discharge of their fiduciary duties.[55]

Private pension funds can be further divided into two groups: employer sponsored pensions and "Taft-Hartley" funds. The former are closely aligned with their sponsoring corporations. The corporations act either as the plan fiduciary or delegate the fiduciary responsibilities to pension fund administrators appointed by the corporation's management. The latter are labor union-sponsored or -controlled pension funds. The union-sponsored funds often cover workers in a given industry (e.g., the Teamsters) and cover multiple employers. Some Taft-Hartley funds have been active on corporate governance issues, but are viewed suspiciously by corporate managers who feel they mix pure ownership issues with larger labor agendas, such as union corporate campaigns to discredit corporate management or representation elections.[56]

Public Pension Plans

Public pension plans are usually defined benefit plans established to provide retirement benefits for state, county or municipal employees. The plans are not governed by ERISA. These plans are generally created and regulated by state statutes which provide some regulatory guidelines on investment duties. As defined benefit plans, if a plan is underfunded, the state or local governmental entity would be responsible to cover the deficiency by collecting the necessary monies through taxes. CalPERS, CalSTRS, SWIB and the NYCRS are large public pension plans which have been identified with shareholder activism.[57]

Prior research has pointed out the heterogeneity within large public plans. Del Guerico and Hawkins in studying the shareholder activism of CalPERS, CalSTRS, CREF, SWIB and NYCRS found that the funds differed in their activist objectives, tactics, and fundamental investment strategies.[58] Romano in her study of 50 large state pension plans found that these plans also differed in their enabling legislation, governing board compositions, structures, and investment strategies. She found that the state plans could be quite "politicized" which affected both the plans investment philosophies and their portfolio returns.[59]

Mutual Funds

Mutual funds, which permit individuals to pursue greater diversification and liquidity, are now a common investment vehicle for individual investors. Mutual funds are closely regulated by federal laws. The Investment Company Act of 1940 restricts the ability of mutual funds to own concentrated equity positions in firms and continue to call themselves diversified funds. SEC guidelines further restrict mutual fund activity if the fund owns 5% or more of a company's equity. The guidelines generally forbid fund managers from joint activities with other funds to control companies. Also, the tax laws penalize mutual funds which are not diversified by subjecting them to double taxation. For the most part, the securities restrictions and tax burdens have prevented mutual funds from actively trying to influence or control the companies in their portfolios.[60]

A growing percentage of mutual fund assets are in individual retirement accounts (IRAs) and 401(k) retirement plans. In these cases, the mutual fund offering the account acts much like a money manager acts vis a vis a public or private pension fund administrator. By their nature and because of substantial tax penalties for early withdrawals, these funds often are invested for long periods of time, which reduces the high liquidity preference attributed to other mutual fund investments. While mutual funds have not been identified as "shareholder activists" they do engage in informal activism and have increased their collective actions with other institutional activists.[61]

Insurance Companies

Insurance companies historically have been major holders of financial instruments. However, they are generally restricted by the state laws from holding large blocks of a company's stock. For example, New York statutes forbid insurance companies to invest more than 20% of their assets in equities, or more than 2% of their total assets in any one company.[62] Insurers' needs for liquidity to pay claims functions also as a constraint on equity ownership. Insurance companies have not generally been identified with institutional activism.[63]

Bank Trusts

Banks are generally restricted under the Glass-Steagall Act from owning more than 5% of the equities of a company. Bank trust companies or departments (bank trusts) are permitted to manage private trust funds. However, the common law "prudent man" rule, which guides trust investments, may restrict bank-managed trust funds from investing no more than 10% in a company's stock. The banks must also maintain "Chinese Walls" between their investing activities and lending activities in order to freely trade the stocks in their portfolios. Bank trusts, like many other institutional investors, also have unique income tax considerations. State or common law generally controls the investment duties of the trustees. Bank trusts have not been identified with institutional activism.[64]

Foundations and Endowments

Due to their eleemosynary activities, foundations and endowments have beneficiaries who are quite different from the beneficiaries of other institutions. Society, it can be argued, is the beneficiary of foundation and endowment activity. These entities are generally exempt from income taxation, although the federal tax code does provide constraints on their activities and investments. Among the institutions usually described as institutional owners, they are the least discussed in the literature. While occasionally identified with corporate governance social policy issues, foundations and endowments have not been identified with institutional shareholder activism.

Constituencies

A distinguishing characteristic among institutional owners is whether the institution's principal constituents have the option to exit: the ability to sell their assets and move, being "mobile." For mutual funds, insurance companies, and bank trusts, if a principal constituent is not satisfied with the performance of the institutional owner, the constituent can simply take its assets elsewhere. Faced with competitive comparisons and pressures for short-term financial returns, institutional owners whose principal constituents are mobile may focus their efforts on maximizing short-term financial returns by trading rather than buying and holding. Institutions with mobile principal constituents will likely establish relationships with the firms in their portfolios in order to obtain information to improve their investment decisions and their short-term performances.

To the contrary, the beneficiaries of private and public pension plans cannot easily move and are often "completely captive" to their institutional owners. Their vested benefits are not generally transportable.[65] Foundations and endowments are generally restricted by their charters to supporting only specified groups of beneficiaries or recipients. Their charters and enabling laws also constrain their pursuit of various activities (e.g., legislative lobbying).

Table 3.1 highlights the differences among the types of institutional owners. A recent study on the effects of governance mechanisms on corporate strategies corroborated the evidence that institutional owner heterogeneity matters. The findings indicated that ownership heterogeneity has conflicting implications for specific corporate strategies, especially product diversification, research and development activities, and firm innovation.[66]

Table 3.1 Differences among Types of Institutional Owners

TYPE	Owners	Purpose	Accountability Standards	Taxation	Principal Constituents
Mutual Funds	Investors	Investment Returns	Securities Laws	Taxable	Mobile
Insurance Companies	Policy Holders	Investment Returns/ Benefits	State Insurance Laws	Taxable	Mobile
Bank Trusts	Beneficiaries/ Investors	Investment Returns/ Preservation of Principal	Trust Laws/ Bank Regulations	Taxable/ Tax Exempt	Mobile
Public Pension Plans	Employees/ Beneficiaries	Retirement Benefits	State Laws	Tax Exempt	Captive
Private Pension Plans	Employees/ Beneficiaries	Retirement Benefits	ERISA (IRS & DOL)	Tax Exempt	Captive
Foundations & Endowments	Society	Eleemosynary	IRS	Tax Exempt	Captive

NOTES

[47] Roe, *Strong Managers, Weak Owners.* Blair, *Ownership and Control.*

[48] Useem, *Investor Capitalism.* Hugh Sherman, Sam Beldona, and Maheshkumar P. Joshi, *Institutional Investors: Four Distinctive Types* (paper presented at annual meeting of the Southern Management Association, New Orleans, Louisiana, 5-10 November 1996). O'Barr and Conley, *Fortune and Folly.*

[49] Diane Del Guercio and Jennifer Hawkins. *The Motivation and Impact of Pension Fund Activism.* (Working Paper, University of Oregon, 1997).

[50] Brickley, Lease, and Smith, "Ownership Structure and Voting on Antitakeover Amendments." Rahul Kochhar and Parthiban David, "Institutional Investors and Firm Innovation: a Test of Competing Hypotheses," *Strategic Management Journal* 17 no. 1(1996): 73-84.

[51] Barnard, "Institutional Investors and the New Corporate Governance."

[52] Brickley, Lease, and Smith, "Ownership Structure." Eakins, "An Empirical Investigation of Monitoring by Institutional Investors." Robert Pozen, while he was the General Counsel for the Fidelity Funds group, wrote an article on the reluctance of mutual funds to pursue shareholder activism. Pozen has subsequently assumed an executive administrative position with the Fidelity Funds. Robert C. Pozen, "Institutional Investors: The Reluctant Activists," *Harvard Business Review* 72 no. 1 (1994): 140-149.

[53] Hawley and Williams, "Corporate Governance in the US."

[54] Useem, *Investor Capitalism.*

[55] Richard H. Koppes and Maureen L. Reilly, "An Ounce of Prevention: Meeting the Fiduciary Duty to Monitor an Index Fund Through Relationship Investing," *The Journal of Corporation Law* 20, no. 3 (1995): 413-449. See also Hawley and Williams, "The Emergence of Fiduciary Capitalism. For a discussion of the "Avon Letters" consult Department of Labor, "Interpretive Bulletin Relating to Written Statements of Investment Policy, Including Proxy Voting Policy and Guidelines," *Code of Federal Regulations* 29: Sec. 2509.94-2 (Washington, D.C., National Archives and Records Administration, 1 July 1998), 318.

[56] Stewart J. Schwab and Randall S. Thomas, "Realigning Corporate Governance: Shareholder Activism by Labor Unions," *Michigan Law Review* 96 no. 4 (1998): 1018-1094. Hawley and Williams, "Corporate Governance in the U.S."

[57] Sunil Wahal, "Pension Fund Activism and Firm Performance," *Journal of Financial & Quantitative Analysis* 31 no. 1 (1996): 1-23.

[58] Del Guercio and Hawkins, *The Motivation and Impact of Pension Fund Activism.*

[59] Romano, "Public Pension Fund Activism."

[60] Pozen, "Institutional Investors: The Reluctant Activists."

[61] Hawley and Williams, "Corporate Governance in the U.S."

[62] Roe, *Strong Managers, Weak Owners.* Blair, *Ownership and Control.*

[63] Brickley, Lease, and Smith, "Ownership Structure." Sherman, Beldona, and Joshi, *Institutional Investors: Four Distinctive Types.*

[64] Ibid. Blair, *Ownership and Control.*

[65] Useem, *Investor Capitalism,* 100.

[66] Robert E. Hoskisson, Michael A. Hitt, Richard A .Johnson, and Wayne Grossman, *Conflicting Voices: The Effects of Ownership Heterogeneity and Internal Governance on Corporate Strategy* (paper presented at annual meeting of the Academy of Management, Boston, Massachusetts, 9-14 August 1996).

CHAPTER 4

Institutional Shareholder Activism

The literature on corporate governance since Berle and Means has generally assumed the separation of ownership and control to be an inevitable attribute of public corporations,[67] causing the research to focus on the consequences of the separation. Within the discussion of the consequences of ownership structure, the proper role of institutional investors and the reduction of agency costs "has spawned a generation of corporate literature."[68] Despite this growing body of literature, the effects of institutional ownership on firm and portfolio performance remains an area in need of further research.

Prior research has exhibited three distinct phases. During the first phase, researchers focused on whether firms are controlled by their managers or controlled by their owners. These studies revealed that the impact of ownership on firm performance was mixed, at best. The next series of studies looked at the size of stockholdings (blocks) and their effects on firm performance. Large shareholders were generally found to add value. Most recently, researchers have begun to examine the effects of institutional owners on a firm's performance. Most activist literature focuses upon specific mechanisms or specific institutions. There is little empirical research which addresses the issue of institutional heterogeneity, activism, and its effects on portfolio performance.[69] Despite calls for finer distinctions between various forms of ownership,[70] most of the research still views institutional owners as a homogeneous group. The literature in each phase is reviewed in detail below.

Ownership Structure

The problems created by the separation of ownership and control are not new issues. Adam Smith in *The Wealth of Nations* first raised questions about the separation of equity from control, and whether corporations could be managed optimally for shareholders. Smith argued that

> [t]he directors of such companies, however, being the managers of other people's money than of their own, it cannot well be expected that they should watch over it with the same anxious vigilance with which the partners in a private copartnery frequently watch over their own.[71]

Before the terms "agency theory" and "agency costs" were coined, Berle and Means also identified the classic agency problem of the separation of ownership and control.

> The separation of ownership from control produces a condition where the interests of owner and of ultimate manager may, and often do, diverge.[72]

The early research, which examined the effects of ownership and control and the Berle and Mean's theorems on firm performance, generally focused on the differences between management-controlled firms and owner-controlled firms. The conflict seemed to be over the definition of a controlling block: what percentage of stock ownership is considered owner-controlled (the size of a block of stock; e.g., whether 5%, 10% or 20%).[73]

The results of the research are mixed, with neither type of ownership determining whether a firm would necessarily perform better. Often the studies did not consider institutional ownership or if they did, the authors lumped all institutions together. Later, Demsetz and Lehn found that relatively small shareholdings (less than 1%) may be enough to exercise significant influence, which casts some doubts as to the appropriateness of block size for classifying ownership control.[74]

Ownership versus control continues to be a subject of research, especially the effects of ownership structure on corporate strategy. For example, in their study of research intensive firms, Hill and Snell found that stock concentration and performance were related, as mediated by a firm's strategy (innovation as proxied by R&D expenditures). This study suggests that corporate governance (here limited to stock ownership concentration) influences profitability through strategic choice (strategy of the firm).[75]

A recent study examined the relationship of ownership structure, specifically large blockholders and institutional equity ownership, and firm risk-taking. These researchers hypothesized that for firms with growth opportunities, the presence of large blockholders and institutional owners positively influences corporate risk-taking. The sample of publicly traded corporations disclosed that only institutional owners positively influenced risk taking. The authors qualified their findings by stating that institutions may not always be effective monitors of firm performance.[76]

Most of the ownership and control literature has concentrated upon owner versus manager-controlled issues, which has relevance to this study. However, the research does not address how owners exercise their powers, and fails to examine the differences among institutional owners.

Large Blockholders

The next round of research, while similar to the ownership and control literature, is framed by the agency perspective. It examines the effects of the presence of large blockholders upon firm performance. Shleifer and Vishny, Demsetz and Lehn, Agrawal and Mandelker, and Zeckhauser and Pound all present both theoretical arguments and empirical evidence for the proposition that large shareholders add value by monitoring the firms in which they invest.[77]

Shleifer and Vishny, using agency theory, examined the effect of the presence of a large minority shareholder. Large shareholders were identified as families, pension plans, banks, insurance companies, and investment funds. The context of the study was takeovers to replace ineffective incumbent management, and the findings indicate that large shareholders play an important role by acting as a monitor themselves or permitting monitoring or discipline by third parties.[78]

Demsetz and Lehn examined the ownership structures of 511 US corporations. They found that the concentrations of ownership of the firms varied considerably. Their study examined the variance in ownership concentration and found firm size and the firm's industry (i.e., regulated or not) affected variance in ownership concentration and the ability to monitor. Their principal findings were that only some large shareholders were effective monitors. They did not find support for the idea that concentration of ownership correlated with profits.[79]

Agrawal and Mandelker studied the effects of large shareholders within the context of the adoption by firms of antitakeover charter amendments. The authors examined 282 firms that had proposed antitakeover charter amendments during the years 1979 to 1985. They examined the relationship between equity ownership by large shareholders and the changes in stock price around the announcement dates of the charter amendment proposals. They found a positive relationship, which supports the active monitoring hypothesis of Demsetz and Shleifer and Vishny.[80]

Zeckhauser and Pound studied the effectiveness of the ongoing presence of large shareholders as effective monitors. They presented a model which revealed the incentives of large shareholders to monitor. A cross-industry study of 286 firms was conducted using a 15% threshold of stock ownership for determining large shareholders. Generally, their findings indicated that the presence of large shareholders improved corporate performance, supporting the idea that shareholders are effective monitors.[81]

Chaganti and Damanpour studied the influence of institutional investors on the capital structure and performance of 80 companies. They found that the size of institutional holdings is significantly related to firm performance, as measured by return on equity. The authors found distinctions between high and low institutional ownership in management-owned firms.[82]

While the foregoing research supports the positive effects of the presence of large blockholders, which supports the presence of large institutional owners, this alone may not be sufficient. The value increases associated with the presence of a large blockholder may not be sustainable unless corporate policy is changed or ineffective management is replaced.[83] The research supports the idea that size of the institutional holdings can affect corporate strategy and ultimately firm performance. However, as is true of prior research, it does not expressly address how owners exercise their powers, and also fails to distinguish the differences among institutional owners.

Institutional Activism

Institutional activism is a relatively new phenomenon, occurring mostly within the last decade, and the relationship between corporate value and institutional activism is still relatively unexplored.[84] Much of the research on the effects of shareholder activism addresses either specific mechanisms or activities, or specific institutions which pursue an activist strategy.

General Monitoring. Under the managerial paradigm, governance matters; the firm is run to maximize the return for the shareholders, who are the bearers of risk. Because equity holders bear the risk of the firm (and reap its profits), they are assumed to have the incentive to monitor the activities of the managers and directors. Prior research has sought to determine if institutional owners, as shareholders, are effective monitors.

Gough in his study of turnarounds and the influence of institutional investors in securing corporate change tried to determine if institutional investors were effective monitors of firm turnaround. Gough classified firms based on the number of restrictions of shareholders' rights which were proposed by management during a seven year period (1987-93). He treated institutional ownership as a proxy for monitoring strength. He used economic value added (EVA) to measure a firm's economic profit. Two hundred nine firms which had a negative EVA for the period 1986-1989 were selected. Then the firms were examined to see if they had positive EVAs for each of the subsequent three years (1991-93). A final sample of 86 firms was identified which exhibited decline and then recovery. Using analysis of variance, Gough found that turnaround performance was significantly enhanced by monitoring strength—that firms which have greater institutional ownership and fewer restrictions on shareholder rights have faster turnarounds. The study assumes ownership concentration in the face of fewer restrictions on shareholder rights equates with power and influence. Gough, as have many others, groups all institutional owners together and treats them as one, assuming that ownership equates with activism.[85]

McConnell and Servaes examined the relationships of corporate value, as measured by Tobin's Q, and the structure (distribution) of equity ownership by insiders, individual shareholders, blockholders (a 5% or more owner), and institutional investors. They studied 1,173 firms in 1976 and 1,093 firms in 1986. Average institutional ownership was 4.65% in 1976 and 37.6% in 1986. Equity ownership was regressed with the performance measure (Tobin's Q). Their findings showed that there was a strong relationship between corporate value and the fraction of shares owned by institutional investors, but insignificant for blockholders.[86]

Eakins examined over 5,000 firms during the period 1985-1988 looking at ownership structure, in particular institutional ownership. Eakins sought to support the institutional monitoring hypothesis which states that ownership will be more concentrated in firms that have higher or more agency costs. Eakins, using agency theory, hypothesized that institutional investments would be lower in firms which are already being monitored by either a large blockholder or as a regulated industry. Eakins used the Brickley, Lease and Smith classification scheme (pressure-sensitive) to analyze the institutions by type. The findings support the hypotheses and generally support the idea that institutions may monitor their investments. The study indicates that not all institutions are monitors.[87]

Daily, Johnson, Ellstrand and Dalton studied institutional stockholdings and shareholder proposal filings of 200 *Fortune 500* companies for the period 1990-1993. Contrary to previous research, they found that institutional investor holdings did not lead to enhanced performance of the firm. Further, the number of shareholder proposals filed in any year was not related to firm performance. The research's overall conclusion was that following an activist stance was not effective.[88]

In a recent survey of equity fund managers (n=206) and institutional owners (n=33), Russell Reynolds Associates found the practice of relationship investing to be widespread among the surveyed equity fund managers. The survey found that nearly half of the managers conveyed their organization's point of view to a board of directors, either verbally or in written form. The survey further found that while most of the responding managers had voted in favor of a shareholder-sponsored resolution (83%), few actually sponsored any shareholder resolutions (9%). The study did not address the issue of the effectiveness of the shareholder activism.[89]

Specific Tactics. There has been some research into the effectiveness of specific shareholder activities. Two types of activism have been the focus of prior research: the filing of shareholder sponsored proposals (covering either corporate governance or social issues), and targeting (the issuance of lists of underperforming companies or boards of directors). The effectiveness of institutional-sponsored proposals as an activist mechanism has been extensively researched, due to the availability of information on the filing and success rates of proposals. Generally, the results of the research on specific tactics have been mixed.

A study by Karpoff, Malatesta, and Walking of the institutional-sponsored proposals filed during the period from March 1986 to October 1990 revealed that proposals have little effect. Neither the *Wall Street Journal* announcement of the proposal's filing, the proxy mailing which contained the proposal, nor the shareholder meeting where the proposal was voted upon had any discernible effect on stock values. Also, average abnormal returns were not related to proposal type or sponsor. Further, no evidence was found that either the filing of the proposals or even their adoption seems to affect either firm policies or stock values. Generally, the study found that contrary to prior thought, shareholder-sponsored governance proposals do not promote value-increasing policies—there is no evidence that they increase firm value, improve operating performance or influence firm policies.[90]

Wahal's study, while speaking in terms of targeting (hit lists), is really another proposal study. It examined the proxy proposal activism of eight large public pension funds over a seven year period (1987-1993).[91] The study was an event study of abnormal returns from the announcement of 306 proposals and found that institutional investors are successful in altering governance structures through the proposal mechanism. However, there were no abnormal returns nor increased long-term stock price performance increases. Further, there were no large improvements in either operating or net income. The findings cast doubt on the efficacy of filing shareholder proposals.[92]

Gordon and Pound examined the activist activities of four institutional owners to determine whether activism improved firm financial performance. The results of the unpublished study were inconclusive, although some support was found that nonnegotiated initiatives, such as proxy proposals, were more effective than friendly or negotiated transactions. The small sample size raises questions about the generalizability of its findings.[93]

Kensinger and Martin examined the stock return performance from 1987 to 1992 of 77 firms targeted by a number of institutional investors. They found no support for long-term rebounds following the institutional owner's targeting. For a smaller sample of firms (n=26), they found an association (no direction) between institutional owners' targeting and improvements in firm performance. The performance improvements occurred following a period of general deterioration. The sample, however, was not random. The companies studied had been identified by the institutional owners (CalPERS and the Wisconsin Investment Board) as having responded positively to the targeting efforts.[94]

There has been little research on relationship investing and its effectiveness. Gordon and Pound in their study of the activism of four institutional owners found that traditional mechanisms (hostile and confrontationary) were more effective than negotiated mechanism of activism, which is akin to relationship investing. Again, however, the small sample size raises questions as to the validity of the findings.[95]

One of the few studies which has examined relationship investing studied the behind-the-scenes activism of TIAA-CREF during the period from 1992 to 1996. TIAA-CREF has been identified as an institution which works closely with management to implement change, and their activities were found to be very effective. TIAA-CREF was able to reach agreement with 95% of the companies it targeted for corporate governance reforms. The changes were achieved without voting on shareholder proposals. While TIAA-CREF has been very successful in achieving governance reforms, the effects of these activities on its portfolio valuation were found to be modest.[96]

Specific Institutions. Other research has addressed specific institutional owners and their activism. An identified leader in institutional activism is the California Public Employees Retirement System (CalPERS). There have been several studies of CalPERS' effect on firm performance. Smith examined the effects of CalPERS activism on firm governance structure, shareholder wealth, and operating performance of 51 firms targeted by CalPERS during the period 1987-1993.[97] Effects on corporate governance structures were merely the success rate which CalPERS achieved in having shareholder proposals adopted and the incidence of management turnover. Shareholder wealth was measured by abnormal returns around the initial public announcements of the targeting. Operating performance was measured using capital expenditures, undistributed cash flow, and asset sales or divestitures. Smith found no effects on stock price, which prompted him to split his sample depending upon whether CalPERS was successful or unsuccessful in having pro-shareholder proposals adopted.

The research also studied possible "spillover" effects of targeting, and CalPERS determinants for targeting a specific company, which included firm size and the percentage of institutional holdings. Smith's findings were mixed and did not lend much support to the efficiency of targeting. There was no evidence of increases in shareholder wealth as measured by operating performance. Only when the success of the adoption of shareholder proposals is factored into the equation did Smith find a positive stock price reaction. Smith's research did support the success of CalPERS in getting proposals adopted and that CalPERS benefitted from its activism—a $19 million increase in firm values from activism which cost only $3.5 million ($500,000 per year).

Nesbitt also examined whether stock returns of companies targeted by CalPERS improved following the targeting—the "CalPERS effect."[98] During the period 1987-92, CalPERS targeted 42 companies to address two issues: (1) poor performance and (2) governance issues including antitakeover devices, excessive executive compensation, and creation of shareholder committees. Shareholder value was measured by excess returns—the difference between the targeted companies' total return and the S&P 500 index total return during the five years prior to and following CalPERS targeting. Nesbitt found that the performance of targeted firms improved following the CalPERS intervention. Nesbitt claims that his study focuses on long-term stock price performance and lends support to the effectiveness of "relational investing."[99] However, nowhere does he define relationship investing and he equates CalPERS targeting and media manipulation with relationship investing, which may be incorrect.

Another leader in shareholder activism is the Council of Institutional Investors (CII). The CII was formed in the mid-1980s, during the height of merger mania in the US financial markets. It is presently a group of public and private pension funds which collectively own over $800 billion in assets within the US. The CII, like other institutional investor organizations, targets underperforming firms and issues a target list. A recent study found that firms listed by CII performed better subsequent to their inclusion.[100] The study examined the 97 firms which appeared on CII target lists for the years 1991 through 1993. The research examined both stock price performance and operating performance (operating cash flows) for the 97 firms for periods before and after their listings. Following their listings, firms averaged a 9% share price increase, which lends support to the efficacy of targeting. The authors claim that the findings also support coordinated or collective activism and quiet governance. However, the public disclosure of target lists may not be "quiet."

In 1986, T. Boone Pickens formed the United Shareholders Association (USA), a non-profit advocacy group for shareholders' rights. Similar to other large shareholder activists, USA developed a target list of underperforming firms. The effectiveness of USA's activism was examined, including its effect on firm value and success in improving the governance structures of the targeted firms. The study examined the shareholder governance proposals sponsored by USA. The findings included abnormal returns following the announcement of a negotiated settlement of a proposal. The study argues that the abnormal returns achieved supported USA's formation, and decries the disbanding of USA in 1993.[101]

Activism and Portfolio Performance. In a study of 50 public pension plans, Romano hypothesized that there would be a relationship between fund activism and fund performance and between fund activism and the fund's board composition. Romano hypothesized that many members of public pension boards are elected and may be prone to politicization, which will lead to activism. The study found no significant relationship between activism and fund performance. The author did, however, find that fund performance was positively related to board independence: the smaller the number of board members who are appointees or elected officials, the higher the fund's return.[102]

Del Guerico and Hawkins studied the filing of shareholder proposals by 5 large institutional owners, CalPERS, CalSTRS, CREF, SWIB and NYCRS during the years from 1987 through 1993. Their results concluded that the pension fund activism was not inconsistent with the funds' goals of value maximization. The effectiveness of the funds' activism was limited, however, to the examination of only shareholder proposal filings and did not include relationship investing mechanisms.[103]

As previously discussed, the relationship investing of TIAA-CREF was found to generate modest portfolio returns. TIAA-CREF has been successful both in terms of adoption of corporate governance reforms and improvements in portfolio performance.[104]

Summary. The institutional activism research has shown mixed results. Generally the effects of activism have been at the firm level, not the institutional level. The research results leave open the questions of whether shareholder activism, and which types of activism, have a positive relationship with fund performance.

In conclusion, the research results on institutional ownership would seem to indicate that the presence of large blockholders generally has a positive effect on company value. The studies indicate that institutional activism is practiced by a number of funds, but the true extent of its use has not been determined. There are mixed results as to the effectiveness of institutional activism; some mechanisms (targeting) work, while others (filing shareholder proposals) apparently do not. The extent of institutional activism and the effectiveness of institutions as activists and monitors merit further study.

NOTES

[67] Bainbridge, "The Politics of Corporate Governance."

[68] Helen Garten, "Institutional Investors and the New Financial Order," *Rutgers Law Review* 44 (1992): 588.

[69] However, see Romano, "Public Pension Fund Activism." Del Guercio and Hawkins, *The Motivation and Impact of Pension Fund Activism*. Willard T. Carleton, James M. Nelson, and Michael S. Weisbach, "The Influence of Institutions on Corporate Governance Through Private Negotiations: Evidence from TIAA-

CREF," *Journal of Finance* 53, no. 4 (1998): 1335-1362, which address large pension fund activism.

[70] William A. McEachern, *Managerial Control and Performance* (Lexington, MA: D.C. Heath and Company, 1975). Rajeswararao Chaganti and Fariborz Damanpour, "Institutional Ownership, Capital Structure and Firm Performance," *Strategic Management Journal* 12 (1991): 479-491.

[71] Adam Smith, *An Inquiry into the Nature and Causes of the Wealth of Nations* (New York: E.P. Dutton & Co, 1931), 233.

[72] Berle and Means, *The Modern Corporation,* 6.

[73] David R. Kamerschen, "The Influence of Ownership and Control on Profit Rates," *The American Economic Review* 58 (1968): 432-447. R. Joseph Monsen, John S. Chiu, and David E. Cooley, "The Effect of Separation of Ownership and Control on the Performance of the Large Firm," *Quarterly Journal of Economics* 82 (1968): 435-451. H. K. Radice, "Control Type, Profitability and Growth in Large Firms: An Empirical Study," *The Economic Journal 81* (1971): 547-562. Peter Holl, "The Effect of Control Type on the Performance of the Firm in the U.K, *The Journal of Industrial Economics* 23, no. 4 (1975): 257-271. Peter Steer and John Cable, "Internal Organization and Profit: An Empirical Analysis of Large U.K. Companies," *The Journal of Industrial Economics* 27, no. 1 (1975): 13-30.

[74] Demsetz and Lehn, "The Structure of Ownership: Causes and Consequences."

[75] Hill and Snell, "External Control, Corporate Strategy, and Firm Performance."

[76] Peter Wright, Stephen P. Ferris, Atulya Sarin, and Vidya Awasthi, "Impact of Corporate Insider, Blockholder, and Institutional Equity Ownership on Firm Risk Taking," *The Academy of Management Journal* 39, no. 2 (1996): 441-463. Chaganti and Damanpour, "Institutional Ownership, Capital Structure and Firm Performance."

[77] Andrei Shleifer and Robert W Vishny,"Large Shareholders and Corporate Control," *Journal of Political Economy* 94 (1986): 461-488. Demsetz and Lehn, "The Structure of Ownership: Causes and Consequences." Anup Agrawal and Gershon N. Mandelker, "Large Shareholders and the Monitoring of Managers: The Case of Antitakeover Charter Amendments," *Journal of Financial and Quantitative Analysis* 25, no. 2 (1990): 143-161.

[78] Shleifer and Vishny, "Large Shareholders and Corporate Control."

[79] Demsetz and Lehn, "The Structure of Ownership: Causes and Consequences."

[80] Agrawal and Mandelker, "Large Shareholders and the Monitoring of Managers." Demsetz, "The Structure of Ownership and the Theory of the Firm." Shleifer and Vishny, "Large Shareholders and Corporate Control."

[81] Richard J. Zeckhauser & John Pound, "Are Large Shareholders Effective Monitors? An Investigation of Share Ownership and Corporate Performance," ed. R. Glenn Hubbard, *Asymmetric Information, Corporate Finance and Investment* (Chicago, IL: The University of Chicago Press,1990) 149-180.

[82] Chaganti and Damanpour, "Institutional Ownership, Capital Structure and Firm Performance."

[83] Michael J. Barclay and Clifford G. Holderness, "Private Benefits from Control of Public Corporations," *Journal of Financial Economics* 25 (1989): 371-395.

[84] Tim C. Opler and Jonathan Sokobin, *Does Coordinated Institutional Activism Work? An Analysis of the Activities of the Council of Institutional Investors* (Working Paper, Ohio State University, 1995) 1-26.

[85] Newell Gough, *Institutional Activists at Poorly Performing Firms: Do They Make a Difference in the Turnaround?* (paper presented at the 15th Annual International Conference of the Strategic Management Society, Mexico City, 1995).

[86] McConnell and Servaes, "Additional Evidence on Equity Ownership and Corporate Value."

[87] Eakins, "An Empirical Investigation of Monitoring by Institutional Investors."

[88] Daily, Johnson, Ellstrand and Dalton, *Institutional Investor Activism: Follow the Leaders?*

[89] Russell Reynolds Associates, *Redefining Corporate Governance: 1995 U.S. Survey of Institutional Investors* (New York: Russell Reynolds Associates,1995).

[90] Jonathan M Karpoff, Paul H. Malatesta, and Ralph A. Walking, *Corporate Governance and Shareholder Initiatives: Empirical Evidence* (Working Paper, Ohio State University, 1996) 26.

[91] Wahal studied the proposal activism of CalPERS, CalSTRS, ColPER, PSERS, TIAA-CREF, FSBA, NYSCR and SWIB. Sunil Wahal, "Pension Fund Activism and Firm Performance," *Journal of Financial & Quantitative Analysis* 31, no.1 (1996): 1-23.

[92] Ibid.

[93] Lilli A. Gordon and John Pound, "Information, Ownership Structure, and Shareholder Voting: Evidence from Shareholder-Sponsored Corporate Governance Proposals," *Journal of Finance* 48 (1993): 697-718.

[94] John W. Kensinger and John D. Martin, *Relationship Investing: What Active Institutional Investors Want from Management* (Morristown, NJ: Financial Executives Research Foundation, Inc., 1996).

[95] Gordon and Pound, "Information, Ownership Structure, and Shareholder Voting."

[96] Carleton, Nelson, and Weisbach, "The Influence of TIAA-CREF on Corporate Governance."

[97] Michael P. Smith, "Shareholder Activism by Institutional Investors: Evidence from CalPERS," *The Journal of Finance* 51, no. 1 (1996): 227-252.

[98] Stephen L. Nesbitt, "Long-term Rewards from Shareholder Activism: A Study of the 'CalPERS Effect,'" *Journal of Applied Corporate Finance* (Winter 1994): 75-80.

[99] Ibid., 80.

[100] Opler and Sokobin, *Does Coordinated Institutional Activism Work?*

[101] Deon Strickland, Kenneth W. Wiles, and Marc Zenner, "A Requiem for the USA: Is Small Shareholder Monitoring Effective?" *Journal of Financial Economics* 40 (1996): 319-338.

[102] Romano, "Public Pension Fund Activism."

[103] Del Guercio and Hawkins, *The Motivation and Impact of Pension Fund Activism.*

[104] Ellen E. Schultz and Susan Warren, "Pension System Ousts Company's Board in Big Victory for Institutional Investors," *The Wall Street Journal,* 29 May 1998: A2. Carleton, Nelson, and Weisbach, "The Influence of TIAA-CREF on Corporate Governance."

CHAPTER 5

Research Questions and Hypotheses

Despite the existing disincentives to monitoring and collective action which theoretically make shareholder activism a losing proposition for institutional owners, at least some of these owners continue to pursue activism. Over the last decade institutions have attempted to alter corporate governance structures, often in the name of protecting shareholder property rights, and to alter firm strategies in the name of improved performance.[105] Previous research calls for the identification of the activities pursued by institutional owners and the determination of whether institutional activism positively or negatively affects firm performance. In response to this call, this book examines the roles of institutional investors and the interrelationships among the predominant players in corporate governance. The following research model (Figure 5.1) graphically depicts these relationships.

Figure 5.1 The Research Model

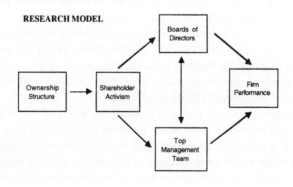

RESEARCH MODEL

The research model portrays the interrelationships among institutional owners, the board of directors, and the top management team and their association with firm performance. The research questions which follow address these interrelationships.

Research Questions

Institutional owners, as major players in US corporate governance, are changing the basic governance structure. Not since the days of the House of Morgan in the early part of this century have institutions possessed the power to control the operations of corporations. Questions remain, however, as to whether the exercise of these powers is associated with superior corporate performance or portfolio performance. The aim of the institutions should be improved firm performance; however, whether their actions are indeed improving performance is still under debate.[106]

Institutions and Their Governance Role

The Berle-Means paradigm offers a focus on market and financial assets. Shareholders are passive investors with a primary concern for financial returns and a fixation on a firm's financial capital. Institutional shareholders, as investors in equity securities and holders of other peoples assets, would have a primary interest in financial appreciation, and income would likely be their major motivational force. The concern with financial returns is likely to cause the owners of a firm to be concerned with its performance and the strategies which mold that performance.[107]

In contrast to the idea that institutions are only investors is the possibility that institutions may be concerned with other than purely financial returns. Corporations use different capitals to create wealth: financial, physical or human, and social or public capital. The ascendancy of institutional investors may reflect a difference or change in the concept of ownership, in which the existence of other forms of capital and other claimants to corporate residual rents are recognized. A financial capital focus may not be paramount, recognizing that human capital and social capital providers are valid claimants.[108]

Institutional owners are responsive to the needs or wants of their beneficiaries or owners, even to the extent of championing their preferences.[109] For example, union sponsored or controlled pension plans may make decisions based upon the creation of jobs, recognizing human capital claims; public pension plans may make decisions based upon the effects upon public interests, public assets, and political gains, recognizing social or public capital claims. Further, institutions, especially pension plans, may consider long-term goals and objectives of society over increased stock prices. These long-term societal interests may include an expanding economy with the creation of economic opportunities and jobs, increased personal wealth, a clean and sustainable environment, an improving infrastructure, technological innovation and the promotion of research and development, and global competitiveness.[110]

There is anecdotal evidence to suggest that institutional owners are not motivated purely by financial returns, but that human and societal capital also influence decision making. Public pension plans and union-based plans are likely to have constituency biases which can inhibit the total commitment to shareholder wealth maximization. This may be especially true when the decision involves the possibilities of lost jobs or lost tax revenues. "Hometown" interests may also affect how decisions are made. These concerns for other capitals may motivate institutions to become involved in the strategic directions of firms: to protect human and societal interests.[111]

There appear to be different motivations, both financial and non-financial, for institutions to involve themselves in corporate governance and the decision making processes. This leads to the first research question:

RESEARCH QUESTION #1: Are institutional owners actively involved in the strategic affairs of companies in their portfolios?

Institutions and the Methods of Influence

Dispersed shareholders, who are faced with the prohibitive costs of any collective action, generally have only one alternative if they are dissatisfied with a firm's performance: exit. A major consequence of the increased holdings by institutional investors is that as their percentage of ownership of firms increases they are confronted with Hirschman's choice: either exit when dissatisfied or influence through voice while remaining within the organization.[112]

Exit is not a viable alternative for many institutions because selling has become increasingly costly. Exit works only if the market is not influenced by the sale of an institution's holdings. As the size of institutions' ownership increases, the exit costs also increase. If exit is functionally blocked, voice becomes the only alternative available to institutional owners.[113] Both the popular press and scholars have indicated that voice has increasingly replaced exit as an institutional shareholder strategy.[114] Voice typically takes the form of shareholder activism.

Institutional shareholder activism can take many forms from extremely open and public to private and behind the scenes, from aggressive and hostile to conciliatory and cooperative. Further, institutional activism can be aimed at either or both the firm's top management team and board of directors. It can be exercised alone or in coalitions with other institutional owners.

At the open and public end, an institutional owner can (1) participate in a proxy contest for control of a company, including board representation; (2) participate in, and often lead, shareholder derivative suits and class actions; (3) steer the filing of shareholder-sponsored governance and social issue proposals; and (4) champion "just vote no" campaigns against board elections and management-sponsored governance measures. The activities can be pursued either individually (e.g., CalPERS) or through associations (e.g., the Council of Institutional Investors). A prevalent activist pursuit is to issue "hit lists" of underperforming firms (referred to as "targeting"), thereby employing the power of the media to sanction managers who are perceived as underachievers.

It appears that institutional activism is uneven, trendy and episodic; some institutions are active, while others remain passive.[115] Anecdotal evidence and some empirical work suggest that different mechanisms of activism are selectively utilized by institutional owners to effectuate the achievement of the institution's goals and objectives. The different forms of activism available, with their abilities to create private as well as public goods, enable institutions to adopt a wide spectrum of activism. This leads to the second research question:

RESEARCH QUESTION #2: When institutional owners are actively involved, which forms of activism do they most often employ?

Activism and Performance

The ultimate question to be addressed by strategy research is what is the effect of an action upon firm performance—specifically, the effect of institutional activism on firm and portfolio performance. There is a general perception of a link between corporate governance and firm performance. Corporate governance influences firm profitability through the strategic choices which boards and managers make.[116] Ayers and Cramton hypothesized that there are distinctions between public/non-negotiated and behind the scenes/negotiated activism and that different returns/gains will be produced when each is utilized.[117] Given the variety of methods which institutions may employ to affect firm performance, and given the responses which companies can make, it is necessary to examine which shareholder activism vehicles are most effective.

An articulated goal of shareholder activism is to improve portfolio performance. If shareholder activism improves firm performance, then portfolio performance should also improve. However, the results of previous research on performance of institutions which engage in shareholder activism are ambiguous, at best. Most prior empirical research has focused upon the effects of specific shareholder activist mechanisms, e.g., the filing of shareholder proposals and the targeting of poor performing firms. Research on the filing of shareholder proposals shows that shareholder-sponsored proposals are generally ineffective.[118] Research on targeting has had mixed results.[119] There is little published empirical research on the effects of relationship investing by institutional owners.[120] The mixed results of prior research leads to the third research question:

> *RESEARCH QUESTION #3:* When institutional owners are actively involved, which forms of institutional activism, if any, are most effective?

Activism and Institutional Type

The heterogeneity of institutional owners may affect the pursuit of shareholder activism and ultimately its effects on portfolio performance. Public pension plans and union-controlled plans may have motivations which differentiate them from other institutions. These motives may spawn shareholder activism.[121] There is anecdotal evidence that union plans in particular may utilize activism to further their collective bargaining objectives.[122] In contrast, private plans, due to economic disincentives of monitoring and agency issues (including conflicts of interest) are not likely to be active. This is especially true if an institution's own performance is based upon relative comparisons with other institutions. The costs incurred for activism and monitoring may lessen total returns which will be reflected in a relative poorer performance rating.[123] These arguments lead to the last research question:

> *RESEARCH QUESTION #4:* Does the type of institution affect its pursuit of shareholder activism?

HYPOTHESES[124]

Institutional Ownership Governance Expectations

Agency costs make it difficult for institutional owners to actively monitor their investments. This in turn makes it burdensome for many institutions to pursue activism. Theory and prior practice indicate that institutional activism is indeed difficult to practice. Economic constraints prevent institutions from active monitoring. Risk reduction, resulting from portfolio diversity and "free walking," and the costs associated with monitoring tend to reduce shareholders' incentives to monitor directly. This is especially true of small shareholders who are likely to "free ride" the monitoring of larger shareholders. In addition, indirect control is difficult. Management controls the proxy resolution process. Institutional owners, due to legal constraints, do not have the ability to be the active monitors of management.[125] Further disincentives to monitoring by institutions are created by legal constraints against collective action. The federal proxy rules, the five percent filing requirements following stock acquisitions, the filing requirements under Hart-Scott-Rodino antitrust laws, the definitions of insiders under the SEC regulations, and the short-swing profit rules are all disincentives to acquiring large blocks and collective action. Also, both constituency statutes and antitakeover statutes which protect incumbent managers exacerbate agency problems, subordinating shareholders' interests to those of management.[126]

The managerial view is historically based upon the assumption that shareholders will exercise their power through voting their shares. Shareholders' voting rights are delineated by state corporation laws. Their voting rights are theoretically quite limited—generally, shareholders have only the rights to elect directors, and ratify or reject certain corporate actions, mostly mergers and other combinations. Proxy fights are extremely costly, and as previously stated, the voting process is controlled by the incumbent managers.[127]

Institutions will pursue activism only if it passes a cost-benefit test, and given the rigors of that test, "activism turns out to be the best strategy in very few cases." All of the constraints and restrictions mentioned above theoretically and practically make institutions "reluctant" activists, at best.[128] These arguments lead to the first null hypothesis:

$H_1 0$: *Institutional owners do not actively attempt to influence the strategies and operations of firms within their portfolios.*

The predominate issues which have arisen are what or who are the appropriate monitors of management behavior. Alternative answers have been proposed, including those external to the corporation (e.g., the market for corporate control, the product markets, and the market for managerial labor) and internal to the corporation (e.g., an effective, independent board of directors, equity ownership by managers, and active shareholders). The problems with external mechanisms have been identified and the effectiveness of internal mechanisms is under considerable debate.[129]

One articulated goal of institutional activism is to improve the performance of investment funds. This is the goal under agency theory, constituency theory, and stewardship theory—only the motivations may differ. If institutional activism improves firm performance, then fund performance will correspondingly be improved; firm performance and fund performance are two sides of the same coin.[130] Arguably, a shareholder will become active in order to receive a benefit. The larger the total benefit to be derived, the more likely the shareholder will undertake the activism. Given the functional unavailability of exit, shareholder activism may be necessary—if not required—to improve fund performance. Koppes and Reilly, perhaps in their self-interest as attorneys for CalPERS, argue that institutions are under a legal obligation to monitor their investments. This is true not only for funds with active investment strategies, but also for funds which utilize passive investment strategies such as indexing.[131]

Much of the current scholarship is looking to ownership structures and the increasing presence of institutional owners as a possible answer. An active role for shareholders is advocated as the answer to any monitoring or control problems, because shareholders as the residual claimants have the greatest incentive to monitor. Admati, Pfleiderer and Zechner have developed an economic model which demonstrates that large shareholder activism is beneficial, despite the problems of free riding.[132] The SEC is proposing new regulations which would relax its constraints against relationship investing. The new rules would permit managers and institutional owners to discuss the advantages (or disadvantages) which would accrue from the adoption of business strategies.[133]

CalPERS, having apparently succeeded in improving the performance of larger firms, has recently begun to monitor and target smaller capitalized firms within its portfolio.[134] An institution should be able to divest a smaller capitalized firm. The exit argument implicit in managerialism fails to explain why an institution would retain the small cap stock. Constituency and stewardship theories, with their implicit recognition that institutions may act in order to do the best possible job, may help to explain this activist behavior. The research of Smith and Nesbitt confirms the success of CalPERS activism.[135] These arguments taken together lead to the following alternative hypothesis:

H_1a: *Institutional investors actively attempt to influence the strategies and performances of the firms in their portfolios.*

Institutional Owner Performance Expectations

Performance Measurement. A major assumption of managerial-ism is that corporations operate to maximize profit for shareholders and that this is desired by all shareholders. Institutions as holders of other peoples monies have a primary obligation to protect those investments and maximize the returns for their owners or beneficiaries. The institutions should be profit maximizers for the benefit of their beneficiaries.[136] Therefore, all institutional owners which have principal constituents which are mobile will measure their performance success in purely financial returns. This suggests the next null hypothesis:

H$_2$0: *Institutional owners that have principal constituents that are mobile will measure performance success exclusively by financial returns.*

Institutions, as previously suggested, may be influenced by their owners or beneficiaries to pursue other than purely financial returns. If the purpose of the corporation is to serve society,[137] then society has an interest in the operations of corporations to see that there is no waste of economic resources. Waste reduces society's wealth and the consequences of inefficient and poor management affect everyone, including employees, creditors, suppliers, customers, and the community.[138] A human and societal focus may influence institutional decision making. There is anecdotal evidence to support this belief. Useem, Romano, and O'Barr and Conley found that the funds they studied, especially public and private pension plans whose constituents are captive, are subject to such influences. The anecdotal evidence has indicated that certain types of institutional owners may measure success by both financial and non-financial measures (a total wealth maximization measure).[139] This leads to the next hypothesis:

H$_2$a: *Institutional owners that have principal constituents that are captive will measure performance success by financial and other returns.*

Performance Differences. Business strategy always asks the question: "So what?" Are there differences between the portfolio performances of the two groups of institutional owners (those that measure performance by financial returns and those which use financial and other returns)? This question addresses the issue of whether the type of institutional owner makes a difference.

Research is beginning to identify institutional heterogeneity. One aspect previously identified, which differentiates the two groups of institutions (captive and mobile) is the ability of their principal constituents to exit. The prior hypotheses in this section differentiated institutions upon their standards for performance measure. There should be differences in the portfolio performances of each group.[140] While recognizing that activism entails a cost, the shareholder activism which envisions a total wealth maximization, not a purely financial return may lead to lesser returns.[141] The following hypothesis seeks to determine if this specific difference is associated with higher portfolio performance.

H_3: *Institutional owners that measure performance success exclusively by financial returns will outperform institutional owners that measure performance success by financial returns and other returns.*

Institutional Owner Governance Effectiveness

Prior research and theory suggest that institutional shareholder activism can take many forms. One type of activism is open and public, often aggressive and hostile. Under the open and public activism, an institutional owner can participate in proxy contests, shareholder derivative and class actions lawsuits, and "just vote no" campaigns; file shareholder-sponsored proposals; and target underperforming firms by issuing "hit lists."[142] Other empirical research previously cited questions the effectiveness of some of these mechanisms, especially the filing of shareholder proposals. Institutions have been advised "not to follow the leaders" such as CalPERS and that the pursuit of activism does not enhance portfolio performance.[143] This evidence suggests the next null hypothesis:

$H_4 0$: *Shareholder activism is not associated with higher portfolio performance.*

Numerous commentators have advocated the use of relational or relationship investing as an answer to the failure of internal control mechanisms.[144] The term "relationship investing" connotes a cooperative rather than antagonistic association between institutional owners and management, both the top management team and the board of directors. A long-term advisory relationship is envisioned with its essence being communication among the parties. It is primarily concerned with the exertion of influence to enhance the quality, independence, and accountability of boards, rather than an aggressive intervention in business decision making. Relationship investing in its simplest form is an established link between a company and one or more of its shareholders. It is also recognized that relationship investing need not be expensive.[145]

Numerous scholars cite the House of Morgan as the model of the effective institutional investor where long-term relationships and stability are created through cooperation and planning. A modern day example of an effective relationship investor is Berkshire-Hathaway run by Warren Buffett. It also enters into long-term, cooperative relationships.

There are shifts in attitudes of corporations toward institutional activism, and managers are creating structures to respond to investors. There is a general movement toward acceptance of the presence of institutions and away from contests or fights. Top corporate managers are cooperating with their institutional owners and establishing structures for increased communication with institutions. Formal and informal communications are taking place between institutional owners and members of the boards of directors and top management teams. Boards of directors and firm managers are openly discussing potential strategic actions with institutional owners. TIAA-CREF's efforts have been shown to be quite successful.[146] This leads to the next alternative hypothesis:

H_4a1: *Relationship mechanisms of shareholder activism are associated with higher portfolio performance than either traditional mechanisms or the non-practice of shareholder activism.*

In Chapter 4 traditional mechanisms of shareholder activism, especially targeting, were identified with enhanced portfolio performance. Gordon and Pound found that these public, hostile, and nonnegotiated initiatives were effective. Smith and Nesbitt found evidence that traditional mechanisms improved the portfolio performance of CalPERS. Opler and Sokobin found that firms targeted by the CII subsequently performed better. Strickland, Wiles and Zenner found that abnormal returns followed the announcements of the settlements of shareholder proposal disputes. While this empirical evidence cannot be termed conclusive, there is considerable evidence that certain types of traditional mechanisms may be effective.[147] This leads to the next alternative (and final) hypothesis:

H_4a2: *Traditional mechanisms of shareholder activism are associated with higher portfolio performance than either relationship mechanisms or the non-practice of shareholder activism.*

This chapter presented 4 research questions and 8 hypotheses drawn from the conflicts in the theory between the managerial and constituency models of corporate governance. The hypotheses were tested using the research methodology to be described in Chapter 6.

NOTES

[105] Daily, Johnson, Ellstrand, and Dalton, *Institutional Investor Activism: Follow the Leaders?* Kensinger and Martin, *Relationship Investing.*

[106] Black, "The Value of Institutional Investor Monitoring." Bernard S. Black, and John C. Coffee, Jr, "Hail Britannia?: Institutional Investor Behavior under Limited Regulation," *Michigan Law Review* 92, no. 7 (1994): 1997-2087.

[107] Hawley, Williams, and Miller, "Getting the Herd to Run: Shareholder Activism at the California Public Employees' Retirement System (CalPERS)."

[108] Blair, *Ownership and Control.* Schlossberger, "A New Model of Business: Dual-Investor Theory." Schwab and Thomas, "Realigning Corporate Governance: Shareholder Activism by Labor Unions."

[109] Garten, "Institutional Investors and the New Financial Order." Rock, "The Logic and (Uncertain) Significance of Institutional Shareholder Activism."

[110] O'Barr and Conley, *Fortune and Folly.* Ira M. Millstein and Lee Smith, *Our Money's Worth: The Report of the Governor's Task Force on Pension Fund Investment* (New York: New York State Industrial Cooperation Council, 1989). Schwab and Thomas, "Realigning Corporate Governance: Shareholder Activism by Labor Unions."

[111] Barnard, "Institutional Investors and the New Corporate Governance." Romano, "Public Pension Fund Activism." O'Barr and Conley, *Fortune and Folly.*

[112] Albert O. Hirschman, *Exit, Voice and Loyalty: Responses to Decline in Firms, Organizations and States,* (Cambridge, MA: Harvard University Press, 1970).

[113] Ibid. Barnard, "Institutional Investors and the New Corporate Governance." Hawley, Williams, and Miller, "Getting the Herd to Run: Shareholder Activism at the California Public Employees' Retirement System (CalPERS)."

[114] Judith H Dobrzynski,. Relationship Investing: A New Shareholder Is Emerging—Patient and Involved. *Business Week,* 15 March 1993, 68-75. Michael C. Jensen, "The Modern Industrial Revolution, Exit and the Failure of Internal Control Systems, *Journal of Finance* 43, No. 3 (1993): 831-880. Rock, "The Logic and (Uncertain) Significance of Institutional Shareholder Activism."

[115] Rock,"The Logic and (Uncertain) Significance of Institutional Shareholder Activism."

[116] Hill and Snell, "External Control, Corporate Strategy, and Firm Performance." Ronald J. Gilson, *Corporate Governance and Economic Efficiency: When Do Institutions Matter?* (Working Paper No. 121, Stanford, CA: Stanford University Law School, 1995) 1-31.

[117] Ayers and Compton, "Relational Investing and Agency Theory."

[118] Karpoff, Malatesta, and Walking, *Corporate Governance and Shareholder Initiatives: Empirical Evidence.* Daily, Johnson, Ellstrand, and Dalton, Institutional Investor Activism: Follow the Leaders? But see Del Guercio and Hawkins, *The Motivation and Impact of Pension Fund Activism.*

[119] Nesbitt, "Long-term Rewards from Shareholder Activism: A Study of the 'Calpers Effect.'" Wahal, "Pension Fund Activism and Firm Performance."

[120] Jill E. Fisch, "Relationship Investing: Will it Happen? Will it Work?" *Ohio State Law Journal* 55, no. 5 (1994): 1009-1048. Robert T. Kleiman, Kevin Nathan, and Joel M. Shulman, "Are There Payoffs for "Patient" Corporate Investors?" *Mergers & Acquisitions* (March/April 1994): 34-41. Carleton, Nelson and Weisbach, "The Influence of TIAA-CREF on Corporate Governance," did find that the relationship investing of TIAA-CREF has been successful.

[121] Del Guercio and Hawkins, *The Motivation and Impact of Pension Fund Activism.* Schwab and Thomas, "Realigning Corporate Governance: Shareholder Activism by Labor Unions."

[122] Joann S. Lublin, "Unions Brandish Stock to Force Change," *The Wall Street Journal,* (17 May 1996): B1,B6.

[123] Fisch, "Relationship Investing: Will It Happen? Will it Work?" Rock, "The Logic and (Uncertain) Significance of Institutional Shareholder Activism."

[124] The conflict identified between the managerial model and the constituency model, and the support espoused in the literature for each model, lends itself to the proposal of alternative hypotheses. Therefore, some of the sets of hypotheses are set up in the alternative.

[125] Alan R. Palmiter, "The Shareholder Proposal Rule: A Failed Experiment in Merit Regulation." *Alabama Law Review* 45 (1994): 879-926.

[126] Ronald J. Gilson and Reinier Kraakman, "Reinventing the Outside Director: An Agenda for Institutional Investors," *Stanford Law Review* 43 (1991): 863–906. Ronald J. Gilson and Reinier Kraakman, "Institutional Investors, Portfolio Performance and Corporate Governance," ed. A. Sametz, *Institutional Investing: The Challenges and Responsibilities of the Twenty-first Century,* (Homewood, IL: Business One Irwin, 1991). Joseph A. Grundfest, "Subordination of American Capital," *Journal of Financial Economics* 27 (1990): 89-114.

[127] Pound, "The Rise of the Political Model of Corporate Governance and Corporate Control." Gordon and Pound, "Information, Ownership Structure, and Shareholder Voting."

[128] Pozen, "Institutional Investors: The Reluctant Activists."

[129] Jensen, "The Modern Industrial Revolution."

[130] Smith, "Shareholder Activism by Institutional Investors: Evidence from CalPERS." Strickland, Wiles, and Zenner, "A Requiem for the USA."

[131] Koppes and Reilly, "An Ounce of Prevention."

[132] Anat R. Admati, Paul Pfleiderer, and Josef Zechner, "Large Shareholder Activism, Risk Sharing, and Financial Market Equilibrium," *Journal of Political Economy* 102, no. 6 (1994): 1097-1130.

[133] Securities and Exchange Commission, Proposed Rule: "Regulation of Takeovers and Security Holder Communications,"File No. S7-28-98 [document on-line] (SEC, 1998); available from http://www.sec.gov/rules/proposed/33-7607a.htm:

[134] Corporate Governance Advisor. *Big Problems at Small Companies for CalPERS*, 4, no. 2 (1996): 29.

[135] Nesbitt, "Long-term Rewards from Shareholder Activism: A Study of the 'CalPERS Effect.'" Smith, "Shareholder Activism by Institutional Investors: Evidence from CalPERS."

[136] Garten, "Institutional Investors and the New Financial Order." Demsetz, "The Structure of Ownership and the Theory of the Firm."

[137] Chester Barnard, *The Function of the Executive* (Cambridge, MA: Harvard University Press, 1938).

[138] Jeffrey N. Gordon, "Institutions as Relational Investors: A New Look at Cumulative Voting," *Columbia Law Review* 94 (1994): 124-198.

[139] Useem, Investor Capitalism. Romano, "Public Pension Fund Activism." O'Barr and Conley, *Fortune and Folly*.

[140] Sherman, Beldona, and Joshi, *Institutional Investors: Four Distinctive Types*. Kochhar and David, "Institutional Investors and Firm Innovation."

[141] Romano found that the politicized public pension plans experienced inferior portfolio returns. Romano, "Public Pension Fund Activism."

[142] Pozen, "Institutional Investors: The Reluctant Activists."

[143] Kensinger, and Martin, *Relationship Investing: What Active Institutional Investors Want from Management.* Daily, Johnson, Ellstrand, and Dalton, *Institutional Investor Activism: Follow the Leaders?*

[144] Jensen, "The Modern Industrial Revolution." Kleiman, Nathan, and Shulman, "Are There Payoffs for "Patient" Corporate Investors?" John H. Matheson and Brent A. Olson, "Corporate Cooperation, Relationship Management and the Trialogical Imperative for Corporate Law," *Minnesota Law Review* 78 (1994): 1443-1491.

[145] Fisch, "Relationship Investing: Will it Happen? Will it Work?" Dobrzynski, "Relationship Investing." Hawley, Williams, and Miller, "Getting the Herd to Run: Shareholder Activism at the California Public Employees' Retirement System (CalPERS)."

[146] Carleton, Nelson and Weisbach, "The Influence of TIAA-CREF on Corporate Governance."

[147] Ibid. Gordon and Pound, *Active Investing in the U.S. Equity Market: Past Performance and Future Prospects.* (Monograph: Gordon Group, Inc., 1993).

Nesbitt, "Long-term Rewards from Shareholder Activism: A Study of the 'CalPERS Effect.' " Opler and Sokobin, *Does Coordinated Institutional Activism Work?* Smith, "Shareholder Activism by Institutional Investors: Evidence from CalPERS". Strickland, Wiles, and Zenner, "A Requiem for the USA."

CHAPTER 6

Research Design and Methodology

Methodology

This chapter explains the methodology utilized to test the hypotheses which were advanced in Chapter Five. The methodology will be described in the following sections: the questionnaire used to collect the data; the selection of the sample of institutional owners; the data collection; the definitions of the dependent and independent variables; and the methodologies which were used to test the data.

The Questionnaire

A questionnaire was the primary vehicle for data collection. The questionnaire was pretested by mailing it to institutional owners located in the Omaha-Lincoln, Nebraska area. The pretest participants were interviewed and their comments were incorporated into the questionnaire. A copy of the initial questionnaire is set out in Appendix A.

The Sample of Institutional Owners

Institutional owners, for purposes of this study, are defined as entities, not natural persons, that either own securities for their own purposes (e.g., foundations, endowments, and insurance companies) or exercise ownership discretion for another person or entity (e.g., pension funds, mutual funds, and bank trusts). This definition mirrors that set out in the Securities Exchange Act of 1934.

Two directories were used to create the sample. *Directory of Pension*

Funds and Their Investment Managers compiles a listing of various institutional owners, including private pension plans, public pension plans, union plans, bank trusts, insurance companies, endowments, and money managers, including mutual funds. *The Foundation Directory* compiles a listing of private foundations located within the United States.[148]

Initially, a random sample of the approximate 7,550 private foundations listed in *The Foundation Directory* was assembled. Upon review of the sample, it was ascertained that most of the sample consisted of small foundations—foundations with assets of less than $25 million (over 80% of the foundations could be classified as small). While the sample reflected the population of private foundations in the United States, such a random sample would not accurately discern differences among foundations as to their size, one of the issues which has been identified with ownership structures and shareholder activism. A review of the lists of other institutional owners in the *Directory of Pension Funds and Their Investment Managers* showed this same phenomenon. For example, most of the public pension plans and private pension plans listed in that directory would also be considered small. Therefore, a stratified sample for each group of institutional owners was necessary. Further, based upon anecdotal evidence, the sample was weighted toward larger organizations. It would seem that larger organizations would more likely practice traditional forms of shareholder activism and relationship investing. As previously discussed, it is believed that the larger plans can more easily absorb the agency costs of shareholder activism.

In attempting to sample insurance companies, a different phenomenon was observed. Most insurance companies do not invest heavily in stocks, if at all. This is due primarily to state insurance law constraints. Therefore, the sample of insurance companies consisted of all insurance companies listed in the *Directory of Pension Funds and Their Investment Managers,* plus a random sample of those companies listed in *Weiss Ratings' Insurance Safety Directory*[149] whose investments consisted of stock holdings which were at least 10% of all assets.

The resulting sample consisted of the following: (1) a random stratified sample of public pension plans, private pension plans including union plans, mutual funds, bank trusts, and endowments, all taken from the *Directory of Pension Plans and Their Investment Managers*; (2) a random stratified sample of foundations taken from *The Foundation Directory*; and (3) all insurance companies listed in the *Directory of Pension Plans and Their Investment Advisors* (*n* = 49) and a random sample of insurance companies from the *Weiss' Ratings Insurance Safety Direc-*

tory whose assets included equities. Table 6.1 describes the various types of institutional owners which are studied and the sources used to determine their inclusion.

Table 6.1 Types of Institutional Owners

Variable	Operationalization	Source
Type of Institutional Owner	Private Pension Plans Public Pension Plans Union Plans Mutual Funds Bank Trusts Endowments	*Directory of Pension Funds and their Managers*
	Insurance Companies	*Directory of Pension Funds and Their Investment Managers,* and *Weiss' Ratings Insurance Safety Directory*
	Foundations	*The Foundation Directory*

The above described sampling procedure produced an initial sample of 954 institutional owners (see Appendix B for the listing of the institutions in this sample).

The mailing of the questionnaire proceeded in four stages. In the first stage, the initial questionnaire was mailed to the sample of 954 institutional owners. In the second stage, a second shortened survey[150] was mailed to a random sample of the initial group's nonrespondents. In the third stage, a new group of institutions was compiled from the lists of the six different types of institutional owners. These 583 institutions were mailed the shortened survey (see Appendix C for the listing of the institutions in the second sample). Due to the lack of available and consistent performance data for the other groups of institutional owners, a sample of 74 large public pension plans was compiled. In the final stage, the 74 large public pension plans were mailed the shortened survey (see Appendix D for a listing of the large public pension plans). The response to the four mailings provided 118 useable responses, an overall response rate of 7.32 percent.

Data Collection

Archival data, primarily news accounts and public financial disclosure documents, are available for determining whether institutional owners pursue traditional forms of shareholder activism.[151] A review of *The Wall Street Journal Indices* (UMI) for the years 1992 - 1997 revealed that most shareholder activism is performed by large public pension plans. A search of various business article databases (*ABI-Inform* and *InfoTrac Search Bank*) further confirmed that almost all shareholder activism is performed by large public pension plans.

Performance data is readily available for large public plans because they publish annual financial reports. These reports disclose the investment performance of the plans and often discuss the plan's investment philosophies and shareholder activism. Each of the large public plans listed in Appendix D was contacted and a copy of its latest annual report was requested. The annual reports of the plans were reviewed to access their investment performance data.

Archival data was reviewed to verify the presence of shareholder activism by the groups of institutional owners. As indicated above, the review showed that almost all activism is reported as being performed by large public pension plans. Phone interviews were also conducted of various institutional owners located in the metropolitan areas of Omaha and Lincoln, Nebraska.

To attempt to detect any non-response bias, a comparison of the early and late responding organizations was performed (Student t-tests).[152] This extrapolation method assumes the late or last responders in a sample are similar to theoretical nonrespondents. The similarities found between early and late responders in a study can be interpreted as suggesting the absence of response bias.[153] The comparison of the present study reveals that there are no significant differences between early and late responders on the variables used to test the hypotheses ($p = <.01$ for the unequal groups).

Definition of the Independent and Dependent Variables

First Set of Alternative Hypotheses

The first set of alternative hypotheses addresses the issue of whether an institutional owner attempts to influence the operations of firms. [$H_1 0$: *Institutional owners do not actively attempt to influence the strategies and operations of firms within their portfolios* and $H_1 a$: *Institutional owners actively attempt to influence the strategies and operations of firms within their portfolios.*] The hypotheses have two variables: (1) institutional owners and (2) the mechanisms for shareholder activism.

Dependent Variable. The dependent variables for these hypotheses are the three types of shareholder activism: traditional mechanisms, relationship investing with boards of directors, and relationship investing with top management teams.

The techniques or mechanisms generally utilized by institutional owners to influence corporate governance and strategic decision making include: (1) participation in proxy contests; (2) participation in shareholder class action lawsuits and shareholder derivative suits; (3) sponsoring and voting upon shareholder proposals, covering both governance issues (such as the abolition of classified boards, the removal of poison pills provisions in charters, and the adoption of confidential voting) and social issues (such as investments in South Africa and Northern Ireland and environmental issues); (4) participation in "just vote no" campaigns; and (5) the issuance of "hit lists" of underperforming firms or boards of directors.[154]

The IRRC annually collects and provides information on a variety of subjects, including corporate governance initiatives by companies and shareholder sponsored proposals, both governance oriented as well as social issue proposals. This source is a primary resource for confirming proposal activity. However, some of IRRC's reports are based upon questionnaire data, and thus only those institutions which respond to the questionnaire are covered in the report. Not all firms which sponsor shareholder proposals are included in the IRRC reports.[155]

Relationship investing is the formal or informal communication(s) among institutional owners and the boards of directors or top management teams of firms in their portfolios to discuss business strategies, corporate governance, or firm performance. Relationship investing in its simplest form is an established link between a company and one or more of its shareholders. Relationship investing can encompass formal mechanisms for direct, ongoing communication with management, or may include merely monitoring the investment's governance structure to assure management does not impede the formal checks of its discretion and tenure. It may also encompass monitoring and intervening in business decisions on a strategic planning level. For example, CalPERS and TIAA-CREF actively monitor firms through on-going and informal contacts with independent board members and the CEO.[156]

A description of each variable comprising the mechanisms of influence including how each is operationalized and its sources are set forth in Table 6.2.

Table 6.2 Mechanisms of Influence

Type	Activities	Operationalization	Source
Traditional Mechanisms	Proxy Contests Law Suits Shareholder Proposals "Just Vote No" Campaigns Targeting	"1" = perform this activitiy and "0"=do not perform this activity	Questionnaire, IRRC Annual Reports, *Wall Street Journal*, and Business Journal Research Databases
Relationship investing with the boards of directors or top management teams	Formal or informal contacts with members of board of directors or top managers	"1"=perform this activity and "0"=do not perform this activity	Questionnaire

The three influencing mechanism variables are operationalized as a dichotomous variables: "1" = perform this activity and "0"= do not perform this activity.

   Independent Variable. The independent variable for the hypotheses is the institutional owner. The description of the sample generally defines institutional owners (see Table 6.1). As indicated there are six major types of institutional owners. Union plans were included as part of private pension plans and foundations and endowments were consolidated. There is support for utilizing only these groups.[157]

Second Set of Alternative Hypotheses

The second set of hypotheses generally addresses the question of investment philosophy. The two alternative hypotheses [$H_2$0: *Institutional owners that have principal constituents that are mobile will measure performance success exclusively by financial returns* and H_2a: *Institutional owners that have principal constituents that are captive will measure performance success by financial and other returns.*] concern the perceptions of the managers about the institutional organization's investment philosophy: do the institutional managers follow an investment policy which is exclusively finance-oriented or a philosophy which considers other factors, such as human or social capital.

Dependent Variable. The dependent variable is the investment philosophy of the institutional owner. The variable is used to identify the measure of performance which considers a variety of factors and capitals. The two types of investment philosophies are described in Table 6.3. The dependent variable (the predominant investment philosophy) is operationalized as a dichotomous variable: "0" = concerned exclusively with financial returns and "1" = concerned with both financial and nonfinancial issues.[158]

Each questionnaire recipient was asked to self-type the philosophy of the institution. The investment directors or chief investment officers of the institutional owners should know the plan's philosophy. Self-typing (a form of self-reporting) within this context should reliably disclose the perceptions of the executives as to the plan's investment philosophy and strategy. Self-typing, as with any self-report measures, can pose reliability problems or common method variance problems.[159] However, the use of a multiple methods approach, utilizing other parts of the questionnaire, interviews and a review of archival data, established the reliability of the measure. Self-typing has been used extensively to identify business strategies, and this prior research supports its use here to determine investment philosophy or strategy.[160]

In examining the large public pension plans, the data was collected from the annual reports of the public plans. It is difficult to characterize a plan as to its investment philosophy from the language in its annual report—whether it follows an exclusive financial return measure or a total wealth maximization measure. One activity which has been identified with total wealth maximization is targeting of investments. Targeting of investments occurs when a plan makes investment decisions based upon where the asset is located and whether that asset has connections to the state where the plan is located. For example, a plan may invest in real estate located in the state where the plan is established; invest in bonds issued by organizations or municipalities which are located in its state of establishment; or buy stocks of firms whose headquarters or facilities are located in its state of establishment. In this way, constituents besides beneficiaries or participants are affected by the investments. Public pension plans were identified as targeters of investments if they explicitly discussed or disclosed their targeted investments in their annual reports.

Independent variable. The definition of institutional owners is the same as that introduced in the first set of hypotheses (see Table 6.1).

Hypothesis Three

The third hypothesis addresses the question of whether institutional owners who are concerned with only the financial performance of their portfolios will out perform those institutions who are concerned with non-financial as well as financial factors, a total wealth maximization perspective [H_3 *Institutional owners that measure performance success exclusively by financial returns will outperform institutional owners that measure performance success by financial returns and other returns.*].

Dependent Variable. This hypothesis introduces a new variable: portfolio return. Portfolio return is earnings on investments, including realized net gains on asset sales, interest and dividend income, as a proportion of total investment holdings, valued at market value.[161]

The data for institutional shareholder activism, investment philosophy, and portfolio return were collected through a questionnaire mailed to the executives or chief investment officers of the institutional owners. These officers should be familiar with the investment activities, philosophies, and returns of the respective institutions. Due to the structure of the study (use of a questionnaire to gather the data because of the difficulty of obtaining archival data), the information was collected from key informants. Because of the difficulty in obtaining even initial responses from most institutions in the sample, no attempt was made to gather the data from multiple informants. The use of single key informants in this type of research is recognized in prior research.[162]

The responses to the questionnaire provided complete performance data for only 18 institutional owners. For this subgroup, portfolio returns were requested for the current year, the fiscal year ending during 1996, and fiscal year ending during 1995, respectively. The variable is an ordinal variable. The questionnaire (see Appendix A) requested the respondents to mark the investment return for each of the time periods. The choices for each period were: (1) less than or equal to 5%; (2) greater than 5% but less than or equal to 10%; (3) greater than 10% but less than or equal to 15%; (4) greater than 15% but less than or equal to 20%; and (5) greater than 20%.

The annual reports of the large public pension plans provide a second database for examining portfolio performance. For the group of large public pension plans, the annual reports use an annualized rate of return which permits comparisons of the portfolio performances. The annualized rate of return for the large public plans were ascertained for the fiscal year ending during 1996 and fiscal year ending during 1995. The variable is continuous.

Independent Variable. The definition of investment philosophy is the same as that introduced in the second set of hypotheses. Table 6.3 provides a description of the dependent and independent variables including how each is operationalized and its sources.

Table 6.3 Portfolio Return and Investment Philosophies

Type	Activities	Operationalization	Source
Investment philosophy	Philosophy that institutional manager will consider exclusively financial returns	"0" = concern with exclusively financial returns	Questionnaire
	Philosophy that institutional manager will consider financial and other returns	"1" = concern with financial and other returns	Questionnaire
Portfolio Return	The overall investment return of an institution's portfolio	Investment return is earnings on investments, including realized net gains on asset sales, interest and dividend income, as a proportion of total investment holdings, valued at market value	Questionnaire Annual reports of public pension plans

Control Variables. In determining the relationship between investment philosophy and portfolio performance, this study controlled for the allocation of assets. Asset allocation (how much the institution invests in stocks) is a factor in fund performance.

". . . the allocation of assets . . . can have a dramatic impact on investment results. In fact, asset allocation decisions overwhelm the impact of individual security selection within a portfolio." *Minnesota State Board of Investment 1996 Annual Report.*[163]

Indexing, the investment of a portion of an institution's assets in a bundle of securities in the attempt to match the general performance of the market, can affect fund performance and, therefore, was controlled for this study.[164]

As the literature review demonstrates, most of the prior empirical research has concentrated upon the activities of a few large institutions. The extent of institutional activism outside of these few large public pension plans, labor union-controlled plans, and coalition firms such as CII and USA, has not been examined. Institutional shareholder activism may not be widespread, and smaller funds have apparently not been studied. The size of an institution has been identified as a possible factor in activism, due generally to the costs of the activism and monitoring. Large institutions are likely to have the necessary size to spread the risk and the expenses of monitoring. Both the anecdotal evidence and the theoretical argument for why institutions may not be activists presented earlier suggest that this study should control for size. For purposes of this study, size is a measurement of the value of the assets in an institution's portfolio at market value.[165]

Fourth Set of Alternative Hypotheses

The fourth set of hypotheses addresses the issue of what types of activism are most effective [H_40: *Shareholder activism is not associated with higher portfolio performance;* H4a1: *Relationship mechanisms of shareholder activism are associated with higher portfolio performance than either traditional mechanisms or the non-practice of shareholder activism; and* H4a2: *Traditional mechanisms of shareholder activism are associated with higher portfolio performance than either relationship mechanisms or the non-practice of shareholder activism.*].

Dependent Variable. The definition of portfolio return is the same as introduced in the third hypothesis.

Independent Variables. The independent variables are the mechanisms of shareholder activism introduced in the first set of hypotheses (see Table 6.2). These are traditional mechanisms, relationship investing with boards of directors, or relationship investing with top management teams.

In reviewing the *Directory of Pension Plans and Their Money Man-*

agers an interesting fact become evident. Many of the institutions in the directory hire outside money managers, and the directory lists the outside managers of each plan. This fact was also described during the interviews with the pre-test participants. Consequently, information regarding an institution's portfolio management were included as part of the questionnaire.

In the typical approach to institutional fund management, the fund administrator outsources the investment functions to external money managers. The fund administrator selects, directs, and monitors the asset management services supplied by money managers, banks, and insurance companies. A large investment fund may hire six or more equity management firms, three or more bond managers, and an investment consultant to monitor investment performance and advise on manager selection. An alternative portfolio management technique is to locate all investment functions "in-house." A number of institutional investors manage all or a portion of their assets in-house (21% of 1,600 funds in a recent sampling).[166]

The focus of this study is not whether institutions should manage their portfolios, but whether internal/external management affects shareholder activism. External management involves delegation to outsiders of the responsibility for both investment decisions and voting. External managers likely vote the stocks managed by them without being monitored by the institutional owners.[167] The delegation of all responsibilities to outsiders would lead to a passivity by the delegating institutional investor. Discussions with institutional investors revealed that the delegating investors do not practice activism, but do expect that their money managers to practice activism.[168] Internal management is treated as an independent variable in the regression analyses of portfolio performance and used as the grouping variable in the comparison of means test.

Control Variables. The control variables used in the analysis of the third hypothesis will also will be used for tests of the fourth set of hypotheses.

Summary

A summary table which describes the independent, dependent, and control variables used for testing each hypothesis is provided (see Table 6.4).

TABLE 6.4 Summary of Variables

Hypothesis	Dependent Variable	Independent Variable	Control Variables
$H_1 0$ $H_1 a$	Mechanisms of activism [traditional or relationship]	Type	
$H_2 0$ $H_2 a$	Investment philosophy	Type	
H_3	Portfolio return	Investment philosophy	Asset allocation Indexing Size Type
$H_4 0$ $H_4 a1$ $H_4 a2$	Portfolio return	Mechanisms of activism [traditional or relationship]	Asset allocation Indexing Size Type

Methods of Analysis

The methods which will be used to analyze the data vary with each set of hypotheses.

For the first and second sets of hypotheses which addresses the issue of institutional owners' activism, frequency tables and a one sample t-test and chi-squares were performed to test for traditional shareholder activism, relationship investing with boards, and relationship investing with top management teams.

The third hypothesis introduces the variables measuring portfolio performance. The performance issues were tested using comparison of means tests and regression analysis. The models used in the regression analysis were of two types. The first tested only the independent variable, controlling only for asset allocation and indexing. These models are designated "Model a." The second type introduced type and size as control variables and are designated as "Model b."

The fourth set of hypotheses will also use comparison of means tests and regression analysis to test the relationships between the mechanisms of shareholder activism and portfolio performance. The models are set up similarly to those used for the third hypothesis.

Finally, the effects of internal or external management of an institution's portfolio upon shareholder activism and portfolio performance were examined. Measures of association, including the chi square and lambda were used.[169]

NOTES

[148] Money Market, *The Directory of Pension Funds and Their Investment Managers*, 25th ed. (Charlottesville, VA: The Money Market Directories, Inc., 1995). Foundation Center, *The Foundation Directory: 1996 Edition*, (New York: The Foundation Center, 1996).

[149] Weiss Rating, *Weiss' Ratings Insurance Safety Directory*, (Palm Beach Gardens, FL: Weiss Publication, Inc.,1996).

[150] The initial questionnaire was shortened following the poor response to the first mailing. It was believed the length of the questionnaire may have contributed to the small response rate. Some sections of the questionnaire were deleted in their entirety (e.g., those questions which dealt with monitoring indexed funds). Other sections were shortened. For example, the sections on traditional shareholder activism and relationship investing were shortened substantially, retaining the gist and spirit of the question, but making it easier for the respondents to answer "yes" or "no" to whether their institution practices either form of activism.

[151] A review of *The Wall Street Journal Indices* (UMI) for the years 1992-1997 revealed that most shareholder activism is performed by large public pension plans. A search of various business article databases (*ABI-Inform* (UMI Co., 1997) and *InfoTrac Search Bank* (Information Access Company, 1997)) further confirmed that almost all shareholder activism is performed by large public pension plans.

[152] J. Scott Armstrong and Terry S. Overton, "Estimating Nonresponse Bias in Mail Surveys," *Journal of Marketing Research* 16 (1977): 396-402.

[153] Morgan P. Miles and Danny R. Arnold, "The Relationship Between Marketing Orientation and Entrepreneurial Orientation," *Entrepreneurship Theory and Practice* 15, no. 4 (1991): 49-65. Jeffrey E. McGee and Michael J. Rubach, "Responding to Increased Environmental Hostility: A Study of the Competitive Behavior of Small Retailers," *Journal of Applied Business Research* 13, no. 1 (1996): 83-94.

[154] Pozen, "Institutional Investors: The Reluctant Activists."

[155] The IRRC annually issues the voting results for significant management and corporate governance shareholder proposals at company annual and special meetings. For example see Investor Responsibility Research Center, *Corporate Governance Service: Voting Results 1993*, (Washington, D.C.: Investor Respon-

sibility Research Center, Inc., 1994). 1-47, and Brenda O. Bateman, *How Institutions Voted on Social Policy Shareholder Resolutions in the 1993 Proxy Season.* (Washington, D.C.: Investor Responsibility Research Center, Inc., 1993) 1.

[156] Dobrzynski, "Relationship Investing." William Taylor, "Can Big Owners Make a Big Difference?" *Harvard Business Review* 68, no. 5 (1990): 70-82. Hawley, Williams, and Miller, "Getting the Herd to Run: Shareholder Activism at the California Public Employees' Retirement System (CalPERS)." Carleton, Nelson, and Weisbach, "The Influence of TIAA-CREF on Corporate Governance."

[157] Useem, *Investor Capitalism.* Sherman, Beldona, and Joshi, *Institutional Investors: Four Distinctive Types.* Kochhar and David, "Institutional Investors and Firm Innovation." Brickley, Lease, and Smith, "Ownership Structure."

[158] Romano, in "Public Pension Fund Activism" utilized a similar operationalization for determining the politicalization of public pension plans.

[159] Philip M. Podsakoff and Dennis W. Organ, "Self-Reports in Organizational Research: Problems and Prospects," *Journal of Management* 12, no. 4 (1986): 531-544.

[160] Stephen M. Shortell and Edward J. Zajac, "Perceptual and Archival Measures of Miles and Snow's Strategic Types: A Comprehensive Assessment of Reliability and Validity," *Academy of Management Journal* 33, no. 4 (1990): 817-832. Nancy M. Carter, Timothy M. Stearns, Paul D. Reynolds, and Brenda A. Miller, "New Venture Strategies: Theory Development with an Empirical Base," *Strategic Management Journal* 15, no. 1 (1994): 21-41.

[161] Romano in "Public Pension Fund Activism" utilized a similar definition for portfolio investment returns.

[162] Nirmalya Kumar, Louis W. Stern, and James C. Anderson, "Conducting Interorganizational Research Using Key Informants," *Academy of Management Journal* 36, no. 6 (1993): 1633- 1651.

[163] Minnesota State Board of Investment, *The 1996 Annual Report of the Minnesota State Board of Investment,* (St. Paul, MN: Minnesota State Board of Investment, 1996).

[164] Del Guerico and Hawkins, *The Motivation and Impact of Pension Fund Activism.*

[165] Romano in "Public Pension Fund Activism" utilized a similar definition for size of the portfolio.

[166] Richard A. Crowell and Robert E. Mainer, "Pension Fund Management: External or Internal?" *Harvard Business Review* 58, no. 6 (1980): 180-182. Daniel J. McConville, "Plan Management," *Pension Management* 31, no. 8 (1995): 6-7.

[167] Useem, *Investor Capitalism.*

[168] Ibid.

[169] Susan B. Gerber and Kristin E. Voelkl, *The SPSS Guide to the New Statistical Analysis of Data,* (New York: Springer-Verlag New York Inc., 1997).

CHAPTER 7

Results and Analysis

This chapter reports the results of the data analyses. The descriptive statistics for the variables are presented first and are followed by the analyses and test results for each hypothesis. As described in Chapter six, performance data was collected from two different sources: the questionnaire, and the annual reports of large public pension plans. Thus, the analyses of the performance data are reported for these two sources.

Descriptive Statistics and Correlation Matrices

Shareholder Activism and Investment Philosophy

Descriptive Statistics. A summary of the descriptive statistics (mean, standard deviation (SD), and valid n) for the variables related to shareholder activism and investment philosophy is provided in Table 7.1.

Table 7.1 Descriptive Statistics
(Shareholder Activism and Investment Philosophy)

Variable	Mean	SD	Valid n
Traditional Mechanisms	.10	.31	115
Relationship investing (R.I.) with boards	.11	.31	115
Relationship investing with top managers	.29	.46	113
Portfolio size	3119.96	8536.18	109
Type of institutional owner	3.99	2.56	116
Investment philosophy	.10	.30	111

The valid number of responses varies because not all portions of the questionnaire were answered by each respondent. The descriptive statistics indicate that few institutional investors practice shareholder activism, and that most follow a financial focused investment philosophy.

Correlation Matrix. The correlation matrix for the variables related to shareholder activism and investment philosophy is presented in Table 7.2. Due to the exploratory nature of the research, a two-tailed test was used for all correlation analyses. No assumptions were made as to the directions of the correlations. The correlation analysis reveals that the practice of traditional mechanisms and relationship investing are significantly correlated (.2557 and .3143). The review of questionnaire responses indicates that few practitioners of traditional mechanisms do only that activity. Most of the responding institutions which practice shareholder activism engage in both traditional activism and relationship investing. Portfolio size, as indicated earlier, is correlated with the practice of activism, as used in this book, especially relationship investing.

Table 7.2 Correlation Coefficients
(Shareholder Activism and Investment Philosophy)

	1.	2.	3.	4.	5.	6.
1 Traditional Mechanisms	1.0000					
2. Relationship Investing with Boards	.2557**	1.0000				
3. Relationship Investing with Top Managers	.3143**	.4735**	1.0000			
4. Portfolio Size	.1514	−.2204*	.2893**	1.0000		
5. Type of Institutional Owner	.0657	−.0458	.1089	−.1326	1.0000	
6. Investment Philosophy	.1758	.0918	.0045	−.0993	.1508	1.0000

$* p < .05 ** p < .01$

Questionnaire Performance Data

Descriptive Statistics. The descriptive statistics for the performance variables of the subgroup of institutions (n = 18) which was derived from the questionnaire are presented in Table 7.3.

Table 7.3 Descriptive Statistics for Questionnaire Subgroup

Variable	Mean	SD	Valid n
Portfolio Return (Current year)	3.40	.51	15
Portfolio Return (FY ended 1996)	3.44	.51	16
Portfolio Return (FY ended 1995)	4.31	.79	16
Equity Allocation % (1996)	.57	.13	13
Equity Allocation % (1995)	.59	.17	13
Indexing	.33	.49	18
Traditional Mechanisms	.10	.31	115
Relationship Investing with Boards	.10	.31	115
Relationship Investing with Top Managers	.29	.46	113
Portfolio Size	3119.96	8536.18	109
Type of Institutional Owner	3.99	2.56	116
Investment Philosophy	.10	.30	111

Correlation Matrix. The correlation matrix for the variables related to portfolio performance for the subgroup of institutions for which performance data was derived from the questionnaire is presented in Table 7.4.

Large Public Plan Performance Data

Descriptive Statistics. The descriptive statistics for the variables related to portfolio performance for the subgroup of large public pension plans are presented in Table 7.5. The results indicate that few public plans expressly addressed targeting (14%). The portfolio returns for the years studied average in double digits. The years studied, 1995 and 1996, were years when the US stock market experienced substantial gains.

Table 7.4 Correlation Coefficients for Questionnaire Subgroup

	1.	2.	3.	4.	5.	6.	7.	8.	9.	10.	11.	12.
1. Return (current yr.)	1.0000											
2. Return (1996)	.8607**	1.0000										
3. Return (1995)	.2333	.2973	1.0000									
4. Allocation (1996)	-.2705	-.2528	.2712	1.0000								
5. Allocation (1995)	-.2710	-.2531	.2709	1.0000**	1.0000							
6. Indexing	-.5774*	-.4229	.0210	.3555	.3557	1.0000						
7. Investment philosophy	.6124*	.5447*	.0130	-.1312	-.1307	-.3419	1.0000					
8. R.I. Boards	-.0680	.4237	-.1955	-.1359	-.1358	-.3419	-.2143	1.0000				
9. R.I. Managers	.4308	.0727	-.2349	-.1359	-.1358	-.4097	.1070	.4708	1.0000			
10.Traditional mechanisms	.1231	.0727	-.0470	.	.	-.1195	.1070	.1070	.3462	1.0000		
11. Size	-.0815	-.1150	-.2854	-.0976	-.0978	.2521	-.1959	-.1398	.1028	.2342	1.0000	
12. Type	.1460	.4999*	.1888	.2532	-.2533	-.4490	.0448	-.1183	.0374	.0862	-.3006	1.0000

$* p < .05 ** p < .01$

". " is printed if a coefficient cannot be computed

Table 7.5 Descriptive Statistics for Large Public Pension Plans

Variable	Mean	SD	Valid n
Traditional mechanisms	.10	.30	63
Portfolio size (1996) ($)	18270770	26592823.5	46
Portfolio size (1995) ($)	13036465	13111947.5	58
Targeting	.14	.35	63
Indexing	.24	.43	63
Portfolio return (1996)	14.86	3.45	41
Portfolio return (1995)	16.81	4.26	42
Equity allocation % (1996)	49.93	14.66	46
Equity allocation % (1995)	45.85	16.67	46

Correlation Matrix. The correlation matrix for the variables related to portfolio performance for the subgroup of large public pension plans is presented in Table 7.6. The analyses reveals that indexing is significantly correlated with portfolio size (1995: .3726 , p = <.05) and the practice of traditional methods of activism. Asset allocation is significantly correlated with portfolio performance (.8453, p = <.01). These findings should not be surprising, and reinforce using these variables as control variables in the regression analyses.

Institutional Owners Governance Expectations

The first set of hypotheses addresses the issue of shareholder activism and whether institutional owners, either through traditional mechanisms and/or relationship investing, attempt to become involved in the strategic affairs of firms in their portfolios.

$H_1 0$: *Institutional owners do not actively attempt to influence the strategies and operations of firms within their portfolios*

$H_1 a$: *Institutional owners actively attempt to influence the strategies and operations of firms within their portfolios.*

The null hypothesis $H_1 0$ is rejected. Some institutions actively attempt to influence the strategies and operations of companies in their portfolios. The frequencies of use of the three types of shareholder

Table 7.6 Correlation Coefficients for Large Public Pension Plans

	1.	2.	3.	4.	5.	6.	7.	8.	9.
1. Traditional mechanisms	1.0000								
2. Portfolio size (1996)	.7651**	1.0000							
3. Portfolio size (1995)	.6757**	.9994**	1.0000						
4. Indexing	.3265**	.3726*	.2206	1.0000					
5. Targeting	.1766	.1736	.2313	.0913	1.0000				
6. Portfolio return (1996)	.2297	.2454	.0542	.3612*	-.0132	1.0000			
7. Portfolio return (1995)	-.1148	-.2308	.1171	-.2525	.1708	.0599	1.0000		
8. % in equities (1996)	.2297	.2470	.1568	.2895	-.0593	.7943**	.0592	1.0000	
9. % in equities (1995)	.2763	.3919*	.1703	.1791	.1896	.8453**	.2699	.9704**	1.0000

* $p < .05$ ** $p < .01$

activism are presented in Tables 7.7 through 7.10. The frequencies were tested using a one sample t-test, and chi-square analysis The frequencies of use do differ, and the differences are all significant (t=3.64). The one sample t-test using SPSS indicated that the significance (the P in SPSS) is less than α =.05, and, thus, the null hypothesis should be rejected.[170] In all cases, the results were the same using both the one sample t-tests and chi-square analysis.

Table 7.7 Frequency Table for Traditional Mechanisms of Institutional Shareholder Activism for Questionnaire Data Institutions

Value Label	Frequency	Percent	Valid Percent	Cum Percent
No = 0	103	87.3	89.6	89.6
Yes = 1	12	10.2	10.4	100.0
Missing	4	2.5		
Total	118	100.0	100.0	

One sample t-test of traditional mechanisms:

	Number of Cases	Mean	SD	SE of Mean
Test Value = 0				
	115	1043	.307	.029

	Mean Difference	t-value	df	2-Tail Significance
	.10	3.64	114	.000

Chi-square test:

Category	Cases Observed	Expected	Residual
No	103	57.50	45.50
Yes	12	57.50	45.50

Chi-Square	df	Significance
72.0087	1	.0000

Table 7.8 Frequency Table for Relationship Investing with Boards of Directors for Questionnaire Data Institutions

Value Label	Frequency	Percent	Valid Percent	Cum Percent
No = 0	103	87.3	89.6	89.6
Yes = 1	12	10.2	10.4	100.0
Missing	3	2.5		
Total	117	100.0	100.0	

One sample t-test of relationship investing with boards of directors:

	Number of Cases	Mean	SD	SE of Mean
Test Value = 0	115	.1043	.307	.029
	Mean Difference	t-value	df	2-Tail Significance
	.10	3.64	114	.000

Chi-square test:

Category	Cases Observed	Expected	Residual
No	103	57.50	45.50
Yes	12	57.50	−45.50

Chi-Square	df	Significance
72.0087	1	.0000

Table 7.9 Frequency Table for Relationship Investing with Top Management Teams for Questionnaire Data Institutions

Value Label	Frequency	Percent	Valid Percent	Cum Percent
No = 0	80	67.8	70.8	70.8
Yes = 1	33	28.0	29.2	100.0
Missing		5	4.2	
Total	118	100.0	100.0	

One sample t-test of relationship investing with top management teams:

	Number of Cases	Mean	SD	SE of Mean
Test Value = 0	113	.2920	.45	.043
	Mean Difference	t-value	df	2-Tail Significance

	.29	6.80	112	.000

Chi-square test:

Category	Cases Observed	Expected	Residual
NO	80	56.50	23.50
YES	33	56.50	−23.50

Chi-Square	df	Significance
19.5487	1	.0000

Table 7.10 Frequency Table for Shareholder Activism of Large Public Pension Plans

Value Label	Frequency		Percent	Valid Percent	Cum Percent
No = 0	57	90.5	90.5	90.5	
Yes = 1	6	9.5	9.5	100.0	
Total	63		100.0	100.0	

One sample t-test for institutional activism of large public pension plans:

	Number of Cases	Mean	SD	SE of Mean
Test Value = 0	63	.1043	.307	.029

	Mean Difference	t-value	df	2-Tail Significance
	.10	3.64	114	.000

Chi-square test:

Category	Cases Observed	Expected	Residual
No	57	31.50	25.50
Yes	6	31.50	−25.50

Chi-Square	df	Significance
41.2857	1	.0000

With the rejection of the null, the alternative hypothesis H_1a is *not rejected*. A significant number of institutions do practice some form of shareholder activism. The frequency tables indicate that 12 institutions, or 10.2%, of the sample acknowledge that they practice traditional mechanisms of shareholder activism, and 12 report that they engage in relationship investing with boards. Both are statistically significant (t=3.64). This finding is consistent with prior research that indicates institutional owners practice some form of shareholder activism.[171] However, the small percentage of use (approximately 10%) also appears consistent with that prior research which indicates involvement of institutional owners is limited.[172] Most importantly, the results indicate that more firms are involved in relationship activism with top managers (33 firms or 28.0% of the sample), than either boards or traditional influence mechanisms. While not an overwhelming number, relationship investing with top managers is considerable, especially when compared to the other forms of activism tested.

Institutional Owner Performance Expectations (Investment Philosophy)

The second set of hypotheses addresses investment philosophies and whether institutional owners measured performance success by purely a financial measure of increased share value, or some measure which considers both financial and other measures. The hypotheses seek to determine if the *type* of institutional owner makes a difference.

> $H_2 0$: *Institutional Owners that have principal constituents that are mobile will measure performance success exclusively by financial returns.*

> $H_2 a$: *Institutional Owners that have principal constituents that are captive will measure performance success by financial returns and other returns.*

The null hypothesis posits that institutional owners whose constituents are mobile (the constituents can move their monies if dissatisfied with portfolio performance) will use a financial measure of success. This group includes mutual funds, bank trusts and insurance companies. The null hypothesis is rejected. A significant number of institutions use a performance measure which uses both financial and other measures (12.5%); the chi square is 13.5000 and is significant (p = <.001). The frequencies of the investment philosophies for institutions whose constituents are mobile are presented in Table 7.11.

Table 7.11 Investment Philosophy of Institutional Owners that have Principal Constituents that are Mobile

Value Label	Frequency	Percent	Valid Percent	Cum Percent
Financial measure =0	21	77.8	87.5	87.5
Financial and Other = 1	3	11.1	12.5	100.0
Missing	3	11.1		
Total	27	100.0	100.0	

One sample t-test of investment philosophy of institutional owners with mobile constituents:

	Number of Cases	Mean	SD	SE of Mean
Test Value = 0	24	1250	.338	.069
	Mean Difference	t-value	df	2-Tail Significance
	.13		1.81	23 .083

Chi-square test:

Category	Cases Observed	Expected	Residual
Financial	21	12.00	9.00
Financial and other	3	12.00	–9.00

Chi-Square	df	Significance
13.5000	1	.0002

In the alternative hypothesis, the institutions whose principal constituents are captive will measure success by financial and other measures. A subsample of 87 institutions (private and public pension plans and foundations and endowments) was so identified. The frequencies were again tested using a one sample t-test and chi-square analysis. The frequencies of the investment philosophies are significant (t=2.95), and the chi square is 56.9767 and is significant (p = <.0001). However, note that these firms overwhelming follow a financial measure of success, opposite of what is hypothesized. Therefore, H_2a is rejected. Table 7.12 provides the frequencies of investment philosophy for the group consisting of institutional owners whose principal constituents are captive.

Table 7.12 Investment Philosophy of Institutional Owners that have Principal Constituents that are Captive

Value Label	Frequency	Percent	Valid Percent	Cum Percent
Financial measure =0	78	87.6	90.7	90.7
Financial and Other = 1	8	9.0	9.3	100.0
Missing	3	3.4		
Total	86	100.0	100.0	

One sample t-test of investment philosophy of institutional owners with captive constituents:

	Number of Cases	Mean	SD	SE of Mean
Test Value = 0	86	.0930	.292	.032

	Mean Difference	t-value	df	2-Tail Significance
	.09	2.95	85	.004

Chi-square test:

Category	Cases Observed	Expected	Residual
Financial	78	43.00	35.00
Financial and other	8	43.00	−35.00

Chi-Square	df	Significance
56.9767	1	.0000

The rejection of both the null and the alternative hypotheses indicate that a significant number of firms use an investment philosophy which measures success by financial and other measures. This philosophy is, however, not confined to only those firms which have principal constituents which are mobile.

Investment Philosophy and Portfolio Performance

The third hypothesis addresses the question of the relationship between investment philosophy and portfolio performance. As described in Chapter Six, two models were run in the regression analysis for each time period: one, with only the investment philosophy (designated as "Model a"), and the second, controlling for size and type (designated as

"Model b"). Also, the portfolio performance was analyzed using data from two sources: the questionnaire and the annual reports of certain large public pension plans.

H_3: *Institutional owners that measure performance success exclusively by financial returns will outperform institutional owners that measure performance success by financial returns and other returns.*

The hypothesis is **rejected.** The comparison of means tests for the questionnaire subgroup shows there are significant differences in portfolio performance when the group is divided according to investment philosophy. However, the mean for the institutions which use financial and other returns is higher, suggesting that a total wealth philosophy is associated with higher performance. The comparison of means tests for the large public pension plan subgroup (using targeting as a proxy for investment philosophy) is not significant. Further, the regression analyses for both groups do not indicate that investment philosophy is a significant variable in explaining portfolio performance. Thus there is no support for the hypothesis that institutions which use a financial measure of success will perform better. The results of the data analysis follow.

Comparison of Means. The questionnaire subgroup was divided into two subsamples: one for organizations which measure performance by financial measures, and the other for organizations which use financial and other measures of performance. In comparing the means for the portfolio returns of the two samples, there are significant differences for the returns for the current year (t=-5.74) and for the fiscal years ending in 1996 (t=-5.20). There is no significant difference in the mean for the year 1995 (t=-.06). The results of the comparison of means are presented in Table 7.13.

Table 7.13 Comparison of Portfolio Returns by Investment Philosophy for the Questionnaire Subgroup

	Return Current Year	Return 1996	Return 1995
Financial Only='0')			
Number of Cases	12	13	13
Mean	3.2500	3.3077	4.3077
SD	.452	.48055	.855
(Financial and Other='1')			
Number of Cases	3	3	3
Mean	4.000	4.000	4.333
SD	.000	.000	.577
df	11	12	4.35
T-value	−5.74	−5.20**	−.06

Regression Analysis. A regression analysis of the relationships of the portfolio performance and investment philosophy was performed. As Table 7.14 reveals, the results were not significant.

Table 7.14 Regression Analysis of Questionnaire Subgroup Performance and Investment Philosophy

	Return Current Yr. Model 1a	Return Current Yr. Model 1b	Return 1996 Model 2a	Return 1996 Model 2b	Return 1995 Model 3a	Return 1995 Model 3b
Size		.215		−.260		−2.813**
Type		−1.264		1.637		−.611
Asset Allocation	.357	.557	−.452	−.384	−.541	−.189
Indexing	−1.493	−1.802	−.453	.502	.898	1.877
Investment philosophy	1.263	.769	1.454	1.851	.718	.727
R^2	.53702	.65160	.33139	−.56507	.17519	.64504
F Statistic	2.70651	1.87023	1.32172	1.55904	.56640	2.18071

**$p < .05$

Comparison of Means. In comparing the means of the large public pension plan subgroup, there were no significant differences in means

for the portfolio returns between organizations which targeted investments and those which did not. This is true for both the fiscal years ending in 1995 (t=.10) or 1996 (t=-1.05). See Table 7.15.

**Table 7.15 Comparison of Portfolio Returns by Investment
Philosophy for the Large Public Pension Plans Subgroup**

	Return 1996	Return 1995
Target Investments ('0'=No)		
Number of Cases	36	34
Mean	14.8800	16.4603
SD	3.558	4.194
Target Investments ('1'=Yes)		
Number of Cases	5	8
Mean	14.7420	18.2900
SD	2.887	4.493
df	5.84	110.08
T-value	.10	−1.05

**$p < .05$

Regression Analysis. Models 1a and 1b for the year 1996 in Table
7.16 are significant. However, asset allocation in the model was a significant predictor of portfolio return, not targeting (t=7.232; t=7.377).

**Table 7.16 Regression Analysis of Portfolio Performance
and Investment Philosophy for the Large Public Pension
Plans Subgroup**

	Return 1996 Model 1a	Return 1996 Model 1b	Return 1995 Model 2a	Return 1995 Model 2b
Size		−1.207		.204
Allocation	7.232**	7.377**	.1.419	1.409
Indexing	.279	.592	−1.084	−1.032
Targeting	.609	.879	.802	.602
R2	.63674	.65165	.12680	.12814
F Statistic	20.44948**	15.90106**	1.35528	.99207

**$p < .05$

Institutional Owner Governance Effectiveness

The fourth set of hypotheses addresses the issue of the relationship between shareholder activism, through either traditional mechanisms or relationship investing, and portfolio performance.

H_40: *Shareholder activism is not associated with higher portfolio performance.*

H_4a1: *Relationship mechanisms of shareholder activism are associated with higher portfolio performance than either traditional mechanisms or the non-practice of shareholder activism.*

H_4a2: *Traditional mechanisms of shareholder activism are associated with higher portfolio performance than either relationship mechanisms or the non-practice of shareholder activism.*

The null hypothesis is **not rejected**. While the hypothesis is not rejected, it is not strongly supported. Only one of the tests (a comparison of means tests for the large public pension plans subgroup for 1996 fiscal year) associates shareholder activism with higher portfolio performance. All the remaining tests, both comparison of means test and regression analysis, support the null. In fact, in the regression analysis for the year 1995, both relationship investing with boards (t=-3.138) and with top management teams (t=-3.138) are significant predictors. Surprisingly, the relationship is negative, suggesting that relationship investing has a significant negative effect on portfolio performance.

For the two alternative hypotheses, except as discussed earlier, there is no significant support for an association between shareholder activism and higher portfolio performance. For the questionnaire subgroup, portfolio returns for firms practicing relationship investing are significantly different than all other firms and negative, suggesting that such activism is associated with lower returns rather than higher returns as hypothesized. This is reinforced by the regression analysis for the same year's data. Therefore, the alternative hypotheses are rejected. The tables demonstrating the tests are set out below.

In analyzing the performance data of the questionnaire subgroup, two tests were run: 1) a comparison of means of portfolio performance and 2) a regression analysis for each activity.

Comparison of means. In the comparison of means tests, there were no significant differences between the groups which practice traditional shareholder activism for any year (t=-.42; =-.26; =-.16). Table 7.17 sets forth the results.

Table 7.17 Comparison of Portfolio Returns by Traditional Shareholder Activism for the Questionnaire Subgroup

	Return Current Year	Return 1996	Return 1995
Traditional Mechanisms ('0'=NO)			
Number of Cases	11	12	12
Mean	3.3636	3.4167	4.3333
SD	.505	.515	.778
Traditional Mechanisms ('1' = YES)			
Number of Cases	4	4	4
Mean	3.500	3.500	4.2500
SD	.577	.577	.957
df	4.79	4.71	4.41
T-value	−.42	−.26	−.16

**p < .05

A comparison of means test of portfolio performance with relationship investing with boards indicated that for the fiscal year ending 1996, there were significant differences in portfolio performance for the two groups (t=3.74). For the other two years, the results are insignificant (t=.23; =.63). The results are set out in Table 7.18.

Table 7.18 Comparison of Portfolio Returns by Relationship Investing with Boards for the Questionnaire Subgroup

	Return Current Year	Return 1996	Return 1995
Relationship Investing with Boards ('0' = NO)			
Number of Cases	12	13	13
Mean	3.4167	3.5385	4.3846
SD	.515	.519	.768

	Return Current Year	Return 1996	Return 1995
Relationship Investing with Boards ('1' = YES)			
Number of Cases	3	3	3
Mean	3.3333	3.0000	4.0000
SD	.577	.000	1.000
df	2.85	12	2.57
T-value	.23	3.74**	.63

**p < .05

The comparison for relationship investing with top management teams, however, is insignificant (t=-1.66; = .89; =-.26). The results of the comparison for relationship investing with top managers and the portfolio performance for the questionnaire subgroup are set out in Table 7.19.

Table 7.19 Comparison of Portfolio Returns by Relationship Investing with Top Management Teams for the Questionnaire Subgroup

	Return Current Year	Return 1996	Return 1995
Relationship Investing with Top Managers ('0' = NO)			
Number of Cases	11	12	12
Mean	3.2727	3.4167	3.4167
SD	.467	.793	.513
Relationship Investing with Top Managers ('1' = YES)			
Number of Cases	4	4	4
Mean	3.750	4.000	3.500
SD	.500	.816	.577
df	5.05	5.05	4.71
T-value	−1.66	.89	−.26

**p < .05

Regression Analysis. The relationship between portfolio performance and the three types of shareholder activism were tested for the
questionnaire subgroup. For the traditional mechanisms of shareholder
activism, none of the models is significant. See Table 7.20. For relationship investing with boards and with top managers, the models for the
current year and the fiscal year ending 1996 were insignificant. However,
for the year ending 1995, when size was entered into the models 2a and
2b, the models are significant. Both types of relational investing became
significant predictor variables (t=7.0085). However the signs of the t-val-
ues are negative. The following three tables set out the results of the regression analysis of the questionnaire subgroup for portfolio
performance and shareholder activism. See Table 7.20 for the traditional
mechanisms; Table 7.21 for relationship investing with boards; and Table
7.22 for relationship investing with top management teams.

**Table 7.20 Regression Analysis of Questionnaire Subgroup for
Portfolio Performance and Traditional Shareholder Activism**

	Return Current Yr. Model 1a	Return Current Yr. Model 1b	Return 1996 Model 2a	Return 1996 Model 2b	Return 1995 Model 3a	Return 1995 Model 3b
Size		.466		–.358		–2.986
Type		–1.552		1.100		–.809
Asset Allocation	1.216	1.338	–.422	–.395	.560	–.225
Indexing	–2.230	–2.755*	–.983	–.151	.706	.1.793
Traditional Mechanisms	Constant	Constant	Constant	Constant	Constant	Constant
R^2	.43153	.61037	.15467	.31662	.12197	.61382
F Statistic	3.03638	2.34980	.82333	.81082	.62510	2.78154

$**p < .05$ $*p < .10$

**Table 7.21 Regression Analysis of Questionnaire Subgroup for
Portfolio Performance andRelationship Investing with Boards**

	Return Current Yr. Model 1a	Return Current Yr. Model 1b	Return 1996 Model 2a	Return 1996 Model 2b	Return 1995 Model 3a	Return 1995 Model 3b
Size		.369		–.537		–4.717**
Type		–1.538		.687		–2.080
Asset Allocation	1.107	1.080	–.505	–.537	.587	–.498
Indexing	–1.963*	–2.562*	–1.865*	–.853	.195	1.226

	Return Current Yr. Model 1a	Return Current Yr. Model 1b	Return 1996 Model 2a	Return 1996 Model 2b	Return 1995 Model 3a	Return 1995 Model 3b
R.I. with boards	−.024	−.507	−2.173*	−1.764	−1.403	−3.138**
R^2	.43157	.62941	.46839	.54688	.29531	.85381
F Statistic	1.177155	1.69839	2.34954	1.44830	1.11753	7.0085**

$**p < .05$ $*p < .10$

Table 7.22 Regression Analysis of Questionnaire Subgroup for Portfolio Performance and Relationship Investing with Top Management Teams

	Return Current Yr. Model 1a	Return Current Yr. Model 1b	Return 1996 Model 2a	Return 1996 Model 2b	Return 1995 Model 3a	Return 1995 Model 3b
Size		.369		−.537		−4.717**
Type		−1.538		.687		−2.080*
Asset Allocation	1.107	1.080	−.505	−.537	−.587	−.498
Indexing	−1.963*	−2.562*	−1.865*	−.327	.195	1.126
R.I. with top managers	−.024	−.507	−2.173*	−1.746	−1.403	−3.138**
R^2	.43157	.62941	.46839	.54688	.29531	.85381
F Statistics	1.77155	1.69839	2.34954	1.44830	1.1175	7.0085**

$**p < .05$ $*p < .10$

Similar tests were performed for the large public pension plan subgroup. Again, there were no significant findings in either of the tests that shareholder activism is associated with higher portfolio performance (see Table 7.23 and Table 7.24).

Table 7.23 Comparison of Portfolio Returns of Large Public Pension Plans Group by Shareholder Activism

	Return 1996	Return 1995
Traditional Mechanisms ('0' = NO)		
Number of Cases	36	39
Mean	14.4825	16.9428
SD	3.349	4.2000
Traditional Mechanisms ('1' = YES)		
Number of Cases	5	3
Mean	17.6040	15.0667
SD	3.206	5.631
df	5.29	2.17
T-value	−2.03*	.57

$**p < .05$ $*p < .10$

Models 1a and 1b of 1996 were significant. However, only asset allocation was a significant predictor of portfolio performance in 1996. In 1995 the models were not significant and there were no significant predictors.

Table 7.24 Regression Analysis of Large Public Pension Plans for Portfolio Performance and Shareholder Activism

	Return 1996 Model 1a	Return 1996 Model 1b	Return 1995 Model 2a	Return 1995 Model 2b
Size		−1.113		.728
Asset Allocation	7.157**	7.071**	1.551	1.635
Indexing	.509	.775	−1.032	−1.002
Traditional mechanisms	−.389	.587	−.062	−.508
R2	.63447	.64731	.10686	.12407
F Statistic	20.25013**	15.60029**	1.11673	.95611

$**p < .05$

The Effects of Institutional Type

The previous hypotheses generally did not address the issue of the type of institutional owner. Research question four (*RESEARCH QUESTION #4*: Does the type of institution affect its pursuit of shareholder activism?) posed the issue of whether the type of institution may have an effect upon any of the relationships which were previously studied.

The results indicate that type of institutional owner is not a good explainer of the dependent variables: shareholder activism (see Table 7.25), relationship investing with boards (see Table 7.26), or relationship investing with top management teams (see Table 4.27). The tests of the frequencies indicates that the variables are not significantly related ($p = <.05$); the lambdas [(.0000) (.0000) and (.27273), respectively] are not useful in predicting activism. A lambda of 0 means the independent variable (type) is not useful in predicting the dependent variables (activism), and none were significant ($p =<.05$). Further in the regression models which tested portfolio performance, type was not a significant predictor.

Table 7.25 Frequency Table for Traditional Shareholder Activism and Type

	Public Plans	Private Plans	Mutual Funds	Insurance Companies	Bank Trusts	Foundations & Endowments	Total
No	23	31	2	9	10	28	**103**
Yes	1	3	2	1	3	2	**12**
Total	24	34	4	10	13	30	**115**

Statistic	Value	ASE1	Val/ASE0	Significance
Lambda :				
symmetric	.01020	.02266	.44760	.65444
with TYPE dependent	.01163	.02585	.44760	.65444
with Traditional mechanisms dependent	.00000			.00000

Table 7.26 Frequency Table for Relationship Investing with Boards and Type

	Public Plans	Private Plans	Mutual Funds	Insurance Companies	Bank Trusts	Foundations & Endowments	Total
No	21	32	2	7	12	29	**103**

	Public Plans	Private Plans	Mutual Funds	Insurance Companies	Bank Trusts	Foundations & Endowments	Total
Yes	3	2	2	3	1	1	12
Total	24	34	4	10	13	30	115

Statistic	Value	ASE1	Val/ASE0	Significance
Lambda :				
symmetric	.01020	.02266	.44760	.65444
with TYPE dependent	.01163	.02585	.44760	.65444
with Relationship Investing with Boards dependent	.00000			.00000

Table 7.27 Frequency Table for Relationship Investing with Top Management Teams and Type

	Public Plans	Private Plans	Mutual Funds	Insurance Companies	Bank Trusts	Foundations & Endowments	Total
No	19	28	1	3	5	24	80
Yes	5	6	3	7	8	4	33
Total	24	34	4	10	13	28	113

Statistic	Value	ASE1	Val/ASE0	Significance
Lambda :				
symmetric	.10256	.06045	1.62213	.10478
with TYPE dependent	.01163	.02585	.83461	.40394
with Relationship Investing with Top Managers dependent	.27273	.13428	1.75551	.07917

Internal Management of Portfolios

In the discussions with the pre-test group and the review of the institutions when the sample was being compiled, it was suggested that many funds do not manage their own assets. The institutions hire outside money managers to handle both the investment and voting of the equities in their portfolios. A consequence of external management of portfolios is the creation of a new tier between the owners of corporations and the corporation's management. The control of the corporation is again separated from the beneficial owners by a second degree, by a new group of agents. In light of this information, the questionnaire was structured to determine if the respondents managed their own assets. Of the firms which responded to the questionnaire, 54.1% hire external managers; the chi square is 72.0087 and is significant (p = <.001). See frequencies of internal management at Table 7.28.

Table 7.28 Frequency Table for Internal Management

INTERNAL (Internal Management of the Institution's Portfolio)

Value Label	Frequency	Percent	Valid Percent	Cum Percent
No = 0	60	50.8	54.1	54.1
Yes = 1	51	43.2	45.9	100.0
Missing	7	6.0		
Total	118	100.0	100.0	

One sample t-test of internal management:

	Number of Cases	Mean	SD	SE of Mean
Test Value = 0	111	.4594	501	.048

	Mean Difference	t-value	df	2-Tail Significance
	.46	9.67	110	.000

Chi-square test:

Category	Cases Observed	Expected	Residual
NO	103	57.50	45.50
YES	12	57.50	–45.50

Chi-Square	df	Significance
72.0087	1	.0000

Internal management and portfolio performance. The relationships between portfolio performance and internal management were tested for both the questionnaire subgroup and the large public pension plan subgroup.

For the questionnaire subgroup, there were no significant findings in either the comparison of means test or in the regression analysis (see Tables 7.29 and 7.30, respectively).

Table 7.29 Comparison of Portfolio Returns by Internal Management for the Questionnaire Subgroup

	Return Current Year	Return 1996	Return 1995
Internal Management ('0' = No)			
Number of Cases	9	103	10
Mean	3.3333	3.4000	4.3000
SD	.500	.516	.823
Internal Management ('1' = Yes			
Number of Cases	5	5	5
Mean	3.500	3.400	4.200
SD	.548	.548	.837
df	10.14	7.67	7.98
T-value	−.60	0.00	.22

**p < .05

Table 7.30 Regression Analysis of the Questionnaire Subgroup for Portfolio Performance and Internal Management

	Return Current Yr. Model 1a	Return Current Yr. Model 1b	Return 1996 Model 2a	Return 1996 Model 2b	Return 1995 Model 3a	Return 1995 Model 3b
Size		.329		−.060		−2.653**
Type		−1.109		−.739		−1.355
Asset Allocation	1.2826	.688	.003	.049	.656	−.057
Indexing	−1.731	−2.112*	−2.163*	−1.584	.266	.131
Internal Management	.599	−.056	−1.414	−1.412	−.173	−1.130
R^2	.45920	.61061	.47619	.52778	.11095	.67179
F Statistic	1.98128	1.56812	2.12122	1.11765	.29118	2.04679

**p < .05   ******p* < .10

The annual reports of the large public plans often discuss whether the plan is managed internally or externally, and a list of the external managers is often supplied. The variable, internal, is used as an independent variable to determine its association with portfolio performance. For the Large Public Pension Plan Group, the comparison of the means based upon the variable, internal management, showed significant differences for the fiscal years ending 1995 (t=3.36) (see Table 7.31).

Table 7.31 Comparison of Portfolio Returns of Large Public Pension Plans Group by Internal Management

	Return 1996	Return 1995
Internal Management ('0' = NO)		
Number of Cases	19	20
Mean	16.5616	17.2035
SD	2.3973	4.254
Internal Management ('1' = YES		
Number of Cases	22	22
Mean	13.3964	16.4500
SD Deviation	3.591	4.330
df	36.82	39.75
T-value	.57	3.36**

**p < .05

In the regression analysis of the relationship between portfolio performance and internal management by large public pension plan subgroup, the models 1a and 1b for 1996 are significant. However, allocation, not internal management, is the significant predictor. See Table 7.32.

Table 7.32 Regression Analysis of Large Public Pension Plans Group for Portfolio Performance and Internal Management

	Return 1996 Model 1a	Return 1996 Model 1b	Return 1995 Model 2a	Return 1995 Model 2b
Size		−1.376		.590
Asset Allocation	6.863**	7.013**	1.431	1.426
Indexing	−.055	.304	−1.106	−1.056
Internal Management	−1.589	−1.829*	−.451	−.520
R^2	.65757	.67564	.11317	.12446
F Statistic	22.40374**	17.70560**	1.19103	.95956

**p < .05   *p < .10

Limitations

Non-response Bias

This study is exploratory in nature. Its design and methodology attempted to move the research beyond the less risky archival and case designs. This study spanned all types and sizes of institutions and utilized a definition of activism which included both traditional and relationship mechanisms. This differentiates this study from other research. However it should be recognized that the sample may suffer from non-response bias. While a post-hoc analysis indicated that there was no response bias, the sample response rate (7.32%) draws into question the validity of the results and their generalizability.

The final sample consisted of 118 institutional owners. The sample on its face is arguably sufficient to study institutional owners and institutional shareholder activism. An underlying assumption of this study, however, is that institutional owners are heterogeneous. The hypotheses either tried to discern differences among the various types of institutional owners or assumed that there were differences. The number of respondents within certain types/groups was quite small: for example, only 10 insurance companies and 13 bank trusts. With these smaller subsamples, it is difficult to generalize the results of the study to specific groups.

The response to the questionnaire was disappointing. This study attempted to flesh out the practice of relationship investing, rather than attempt an archival study of traditional mechanisms of activism. In so doing, it relied upon questionnaire responses and interviews for data collection. There is an apparent reluctance on the part of many institutional owners to answer such questionnaires. Some of the institutions contacted refused to even discuss their voting and investment philosophies.

Time Limit

Another limitation on the interpretation of portfolio performance is the time frame for this study. With regard to the scope of this study, it examined only shareholder activism and portfolio performance since 1995. The time frame was restricted to this period due to the data collection method chosen—a questionnaire. A respondent's recollection of past activities is questionable if asked to recollect activities which occurred more than one year ago.[173] While the performance and investment data is archival and can be reconstructed, the questions regarding shareholder activism and relationship investing necessitate a "current" time frame. Secondly, the portfolio returns were found to be significantly affected by asset allocation (see Table 7.24). The stock market performances during the years 1995 and 1996 were generally quite good. This factor more than any other could have equalized portfolio returns. All funds which were substantially in the market experienced above average returns, which may have overshadowed any returns allocable to shareholder activism.

Also, this study is cross-sectional. It examines phenomena which may be subject to time effects. Shareholder activism practiced today may not have an effect on a company's strategies, performance or governance for a number of years. Therefore, this limits the inferences which can be drawn from this study's findings. This study, however, does provide a beginning for future longitudinal work.

Methodology

Finally, this study, by its chosen methodology, restricts the inferences which can be drawn from the results. This study examined associations among various variables. The direction of the associations cannot be clearly made.

The results presented in this chapter generally confirm that shareholder activism is not widespread; financial measures of performance predominate and portfolio performance is not positively affected by activism. It is interesting to note that, due to the inclusion of relationship investing tactics, the percentage of respondents who report any form of activism in this study is significantly higher than that found in other studies.[174] The implications of the findings for institutional managers, corporate managers, regulators and future research will be discussed in chapter eight.

NOTES

[170] Gerber and Voelkl, *The SPSS Guide*.

[171] Russell Reynolds Associates, *Redefining Corporate Governance*.

[172] Kensinger and Martin, *Relationship Investing: What Active Institutional Investors Want from Management*.

[173] Floyd J. Fowler, Jr., *Improving Survey Questions: Design and Evaluation*, (Thousand Oaks, CA: Sage Publications, 1995).

[174] Daily, Johnson, Ellstrand, and Dalton, *Institutional Investor Activism: Follow the Leaders?*

CHAPTER 8

Implications for Institutions, Corporations, Regulators and Future Research

.. as a shareholder, the SBI [State Board of Investments] can participate in shaping corporate policies and practices." *Minnesota State
Board of Investment 1996 Annual Report*[75]

Institutional owners have a major ownership presence in United States
corporate governance. This presence will not likely decrease in the future; it will only increase as investors move more money into mutual
funds and retirement savings become more concentrated in pension
plans, both private and public. If the social security system, or any part of
it, is privatized, then the power of institutional owners will further increase. When this study was initially proposed, the popular press was reporting the increasing activism of institutional owners and the effects of
this activism on firm operations, decision making, and performance.
Such reporting is continuing, and institutional shareholder activism has
been characterized as "on a roll" succeeding in transforming the boards
and corporate governance policies of numerous companies.[176]

This study was initiated to examine how widespread are the phenomena of shareholder activism and relationship investing, and if widespread, why institutional owners pursue such activism. These questions
were not previously addressed in a broad-based study of institutional
ownership. In addressing new questions, this study is exploratory in
nature.

The results support some hypotheses, while others are not supported. Table 8.1 is a summary of the results of the hypotheses tests. The
analysis of the results as they pertain to each hypothesis follow.

Table 8.1 Summary of Hypotheses Results

$H_1 0$: *Institutional owners do not actively attempt to influence the strategies and operations of firms within their portfolios.*   ***Rejected***

$H_1 a$: *Institutional owners actively attempt to influence the strategies and operations of firms within their portfolios.*   ***Not Rejected***

$H_2 0$: *Institutional owners that have principal constituents that are mobile will measure performance success exclusively by financial returns.*   ***Rejected***

$H_2 a$: *Institutional owners that have principal constituents that are captive will measure performance success by financial returns and other returns.*   ***Rejected***

H_3: *Institutional owners that measure performance success exclusively by financial returns will outperform institutional owners that measure performance success by financial returns and other returns.*   ***Rejected***

$H_4 0$: *Shareholder activism is not associated with higher portfolio performance*   ***Not Rejected***

$H_4 a1$: *Relationship mechanisms of shareholder activism are associated with higher portfolio performance than either traditional mechanisms or the non-practice of shareholder activism.*   ***Rejected***

$H_4 a2$: *Traditional mechanisms of shareholder activism are associated with higher portfolio performance than either relationship mechanisms or the non-practice of shareholder activism*   ***Rejected***

Breadth of Activism (Institutional Owner Governance Expectations)

The first two research questions posed in Chapter five addressed the fundamental issue of the breadth or extent of shareholder activism[177] Some prior research had indicated that the practice of "traditional" shareholder activism may be quite limited.[178] A review of the financial and legal literature indicates that most reporting of institutional shareholder activism is centered on a few large public or private pension plans, especially the activism of CalPERS and TIAA-CREF. This study's findings support the prior research and anecdotal evidence which indicate that the use of traditional mechanisms of shareholder activism is not widespread. Approximately 10% of the respondents practice traditional shareholder activism, and an even smaller number practice only this type of activism. This "non-use" of traditional mechanisms is not restricted to any type of institution. Public pension plans and union plans, which have historically been identified with traditional activism, in their responses to the questionnaire did not indicate that they are practitioners of traditional mechanisms.

While the research supports the idea that the practice of traditional shareholder activism is not widespread, the same is not true for relationship investing. Relationship investing is broadly defined in this study to include any interactions with members of the boards of directors and top management teams of the companies in an institution's portfolio to discuss the firm's performance, business strategies, and/or corporate governance. Similar to traditional shareholder mechanisms, relationship investing with boards is not widespread. However, almost 30% of the responding institutional owners practice relationship investing with top management teams. Relationship investing is practiced by more institutional owners than traditional methods of activism. This supports the prior evidence of the increasing use of relationship investing.[179] The practice seems to be especially prevalent among firms which manage some or all of their portfolios internally.

It appears that most institutional owners practice neither traditional shareholder activism nor relationship investing. Those which do so are likely to be those institutional owners which manage their own funds. A number of institutions contacted indicated that while they did not practice shareholder activism or relationship investing, they believed that the external money managers they employ may entertain such practices and that the institutional owners would expect their external managers to pursue those activities.

Institutional Owner Investment Philosophies

The first research question also implicitly addressed the broader issue of why institutional owners would practice shareholder activism.[180] It is argued that institutional owners practice shareholder activism to improve the performance of their portfolios. However, portfolio returns are not the only measure of improved performance. While managerialism argues for purely financial measures, constituency and stewardship theories look toward total wealth maximization utilizing both financial and other measures. While many responding institutions indicated that they measure performance by a purely financial measure, the number which use a combination of financial and non-financial measures is statistically significant.

Romano (1993) argued that pension plans, especially the "politicized" public plans, would invest not purely to maximize financial wealth.[181] They would maximize total wealth through the targeting of investments to the localities where the plans were located. Targeting would thus evidence a combination measurement philosophy. Interestingly, only two respondents indicated that they targeted investments. This is despite the fact that public pension plans are often granted the authority to invest in assets with ties to their locales. While large public plans are identified as the type of plans which would most likely be pressured to target investments, no large public plans which responded to the survey indicated that they target investments. A review of the annual reports of the large public plans revealed that few plans (14%) even explicitly discuss or address targeting of their investments.

Financial motivations predominate. It appears that most institutions practice shareholder activism to improve portfolio performance and thus improve financial performance. This should not be surprising, because both common law (the prudent man rule) and ERISA arguably mandate a pure financial motivation philosophy for many institutional owners. However, there is evidence that some institutions do use performance measures which recognize other measures, which lends support to the idea that there are institutional owners that may recognize other than financial capitals and residual claimants other than shareholders/owners.

Institutional Owner Performance Expectations

The third research question broadly addressed the issue of the effectiveness of shareholder activism.[182] It assumes that shareholder activism, whether traditional or relationship, will positively affect portfolio performance. Little support was found for the association of shareholder activism and portfolio performance.

In testing hypothesis three, which posits that firms which measure success exclusively by financial measures will be associated with higher performance, the findings did not support the hypothesis. Neither a financial maximization nor a total wealth maximization philosophy was associated with better performance.

The fourth set of hypotheses tested whether shareholder activism, either traditional or relationship, is associated with higher portfolio performance. The results indicate that neither traditional shareholder activism nor relationship investing, whether with boards or top management teams, are associated with higher portfolio performance. Perhaps the most interesting finding of this study was the negative effects of relationship investing on portfolio performance. This finding casts some doubt on the common wisdom that firms should practice relationship investing to improve portfolio performance.

The Effects of Institutional Type

The last research question addressed the issue of whether the type of institution makes a difference.[183] The second set of hypotheses examined whether there was a relationship between type and investment philosophy. None was found. The third hypothesis examined whether investment philosophy and portfolio performance were related. They are not. There is not a significant finding that either an exclusive financial measure of success or a combination of financial and other measures was superior. The evidence is not conclusive. With regard to whether type generally affected portfolio performance, in none of the regression models was type a significant determinant of portfolio performance.

With respect to the practice of shareholder activism, no one type dominated either traditional activism or relationship investing with boards. It appears that firms which have constituents that are mobile may be more prone to practice relationship investing with top management teams.

Implications for Institutional Owners and Corporate Managers

The study has implications for both institutional owners and the corporations whose stock they hold in their portfolios. A surprising finding was the negative relationship between relational investing and portfolio performance, found in two of the regression models. This has significant implications for institutional owners, and draws into question the wisdom of relationship investing, and the justification for its practice that it improves portfolio performance. The activities of TIAA-CREF encompass both traditional and relationship mechanisms. While TIAA-CREF has been successful in achieving corporate governance policy reforms, the success of its activism on portfolio returns was described as modest.[184] Further research is necessary to determine if relationship investing leads to better, or worse, portfolio performance.

There is considerable debate over the effectiveness of shareholder activism. Recent empirical research casts doubt on the effectiveness of traditional mechanisms of influence.[185] The literature review reveals that the efficacy of many forms of activism is questionable. The results support the research which questions the effectiveness of shareholder activism. The findings call into question the policies of institutions which expend resources to actively monitor the strategies and governance of the firms in their portfolios. There is some evidence that targeting is effective.[186] However, targeting usually earmarks only a small number of firms (e.g., CalPERS list of 50 underperforming companies) in a portfolio which includes equities of hundreds of firms. The question remains whether shareholder activism in toto, both traditional and relationship, is effective. Further research is necessary to determine whether the finding that relationship investing has a negative effect on portfolio performance is evident in other samples of institutional owners or in the activities of other than large pension funds. Additional research is required to clarify the use of shareholder activism, especially relationship investing with top managers, and the interrelationships between the top managers of corporations and their institutional owners.

Generally, this study found that shareholder activism, whether traditional or relationship, is not a widespread phenomenon. The author anticipated that more institutions would indicate that they practice some form of activism. Most responding institutional owners do not practice either form of activism. This finding has practical implications for corporate managers. While corporate governance issues will continue to confront managers, there is no apparent groundswell by institutional owners to utilize these methods to challenge management strategies or decisions.

It appears that some institutional activists may even be retreating from their confrontational past. Numerous studies have examined the filing of shareholder proposals and the voting of shareholder proposals. For example, CalSTERS, once identified as an activist institutional owner, recently reported that it had not filed any shareholder proposals, and in a recent proxy season sided with management on the majority of the votes and issues in the proxies of over 4,200 corporations.[187] While managers are not free to ignore their institutional owners, the great fears of an impending movement to institutional meddling is not supported.

The ownership of corporations will continue to be concentrated in the hands of institutional owners. As institutions own more shares, both domestically and internationally, exit may indeed be foreclosed. Voice in the realm of shareholder activism, especially relationship investing, may be a likely response. This may be especially true for those institutions that have principal constituents which are mobile. There is still a perception that relationship investing is worthwhile. Further research is necessary to determine the effects of relationship investing on institutional portfolio performance and on corporate strategies and decision making.

Implications for Theory

Two areas were not expressly addressed by either the research questions or the hypotheses. These are institutional heterogeneity and the internal management of institutional portfolios.

Institutional Heterogeneity

It is argued earlier in this book, though not hypothesized, that rather than the accepted view of institutional homogeneity, institutional owners are actually heterogeneous. As previously noted, in much of the management literature, institutional owners have been perceived as one homogeneous group. The results of the study lend support to the theory of institutional heterogeneity.

The past and current literature have classified institutional owners into various groups.[188] This study follows this trend and categorizes the institutions into six groups. The findings indicate that institutions are different. They differ in their pursuit of activism (H_1a). They differ in investment philosophy ($H_2 0$). The differences are evident even among the institutions that have principal constituents which are captive.

These findings, together with the fundamental differences identified earlier, confirm institutional heterogeneity. A major contribution of this book is its support for the view of institutional heterogeneity. It can no longer be presumed that institutional owners/investors act alike. Institutional heterogeneity should guide future research. The differences among institutional owners should be addressed, especially the differences in investment philosophies, to discern both their effects on portfolio performance and on corporate strategies, governance, and decision making.

Internal Management of Portfolios

In both the questionnaire and reviews of the public pension plan annual reports, an additional research issue was pursued. Do institutional owners manage the assets in their portfolios and what is the effect of internal management on shareholder activism and corporate governance in general?

Institutions which manage their own assets have the ability as shareholders to participate in corporate governance. However, when those institutions hire external managers, they often relinquish the voting power of their stocks. It appears that the external managers often vote the proxies without being monitored by their institutional owners.[189]

If institutions do not manage their own funds, are we studying the wrong groups? The real money managers—mutual funds, insurance companies, and bank trusts—not all institutional owners, may be the firms which should be examined with respect to the exercise of institutional ownership power. Black (1992) characterized institutional owners as "agents watching other agents."[190] However, through the prevalent use of external fund managers (paid agents) what is created is a situation of "agents watching agents watching agents": the institutions watch over their fund managers who are monitoring the boards and managers of the entities in the portfolios. Figure 8.1 depicts this phenomenon of the multiple relationships among institutional owners, other shareholders, the money managers, and the managers of corporations (both boards of directors and top management teams).

Figure 8.1 "Agents Watching Agents Watching Agents"

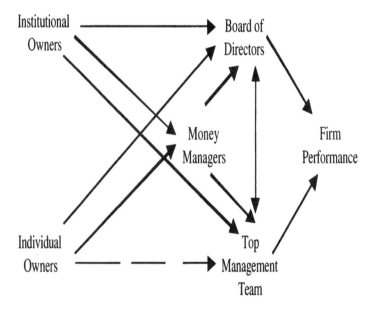

Current research in connection with institutional ownership may be examining the wrong relationships and looking at the wrong groups. Brickley, Lease and Smith classified institutional owners on the basis of their sensitivity to the potential loss of business revenues if they practiced shareholder activism. Institutions which could potentially lose business or which were confronted by this conflict of interests were dubbed "pressure sensitive."[191] However, under external management, if it is the money managers which hold the voting power and which are confronted with conflicts of interests, then the wrong parties are being studied. The Brickley, Lease and Smith taxonomy may be incorrect. Future research should study the relationships among money managers, institutional owners, and the corporations which are owned.

The findings also suggest that internal management is a strong explainer of shareholder activism. Future research should endeavor to verify whether internal management is a determinant of shareholder activism.

Other Theoretical Implications.

As indicated earlier, a surprising finding was the negative association between relationship investing and portfolio performance. This also has implications for theory. Agency theory identifies the costs inherent in shareholder monitoring and activism. Future studies may be able to clarify the associations between relationship investing and portfolio performance, and whether agency theory is the proper framework for such studies.

It appears that size of institution has an effect upon shareholder activism and may have an effect on portfolio performance.[192] Portfolio size, as indicated earlier, is correlated with the practice of activism, especially relationship investing (see tables 7.2 and 7.6). While size was not directly addressed in this study, its presence was controlled for in the models. Anecdotal evidence continues to raise the issue of whether the size of the institution is related to the practice of institutional shareholder activism. It is left to future studies to pursue further this association.

This study identified the presence of private relationships among institutional owners, money managers, and top management teams, and that these relationships may have performance effects. Research using archival data will not fully reveal these relationships and their effects on firm strategies and firm performance. It is important to pursue these questions, not relying solely upon secondary data sources.

This book is an exploratory study of institutional ownership and its effects on corporations. It identified a moderate use by firms of relationship investing with top management teams. It supported the growing view that institutional owners are heterogeneous in many respects. Further, it identified internal management of institutional portfolios as a potential determinant for institutional shareholder activism and institutional shareholder influence. Future research will be necessary to more definitively answer the questions which were posed within this study.

Implications for Regulation

The legal literature in particular has addressed the issue of whether there is sufficient regulation of institutional owner activism.[193] The results herein indicate that institutional activism is not widespread. The fears that institutional owners have become meddlers in the internal affairs of corporations does not appear to be occurring. The issues examined by this study do not support a call for further regulation to control the activities of institutional owners.

For firms which practice only relationship investing, the most prevalent users are firms which are previously identified as being pressure-sensitive owners, e.g., mutual funds, insurance companies, and bank trusts. These types of institutional owners are also identified as those that have principal constituents which are mobile. A question left unanswered by the research is the extent to which relationship investing may be a mechanism to attain non-public information which will benefit the institutional or money fund managers, whose success is measured by whether they have satisfied their mobile constituents. Future research should address the question whether large shareholders which practice activism do so to the detriment of smaller shareholders.

Conclusion

The ownership structure of corporations is changing due to the increased stock ownership by institutions. In tandem with this growth of institutional ownership has been the emergence of shareholder activism. This book analyzed shareholder activism, both the traditional mechanisms of influence (e.g., filing of shareholder proposals) and relationship investing (a long-term and cooperative arrangement where owners seek a voice in determining business strategies and governance). This book examined the breadth of activism, the reasons behind institutional activism, and the effects of activism on institutional portfolio performance.

The findings indicate that there is little breadth to institutional shareholder activism. Most of the institutions which responded to the questionnaire do not practice either traditional mechanisms of influence or relationship investing. Some firms (about 30%) practice relationship investing with top managers. Most institutions typed themselves as followers of a finance-oriented investment philosophy, not a total wealth, investment philosophy. However, the study supports the recent anecdotal evidence which indicates that some institutions pursue a total wealth maximization philosophy—that wealth is created not only by financial capital but also by human and social capital. With respect to portfolio performance, the findings indicate that shareholder activism is not associated with higher performance. Most interesting was the finding that relationship investing, both with boards and top managers, had a negative effect on portfolio returns of the institutions studied. The type of institutional owner seemingly does not make a difference.

In researching institution activism, additional issues arose, including the effects of who manages an institution's portfolio. Internal management is identified as a possible determinant of activism. This study also identifies money managers as potential sources of power in US corporate governance. These issues further reflect the changing ownership structure of corporations. What this book ultimately confirms is that the increasing presence of institutional owners and their possible effects on corporate governance will continue to be a fruitful area for research which has both theoretical and practical implications.

NOTES

[175] Minnesota State Board of Investment, *The 1996 Annual Report*.

[176] Schultz and Warren, "Big Victory for Institutional Investors."

[177] *Research Question #1* : Are institutional owners actively involved in the strategic affairs of companies in their portfolios? and *Research Question #2* : When institutional owners are actively involved, which forms of activism do they most often employ?

[178] Kensinger and Martin, *Relationship Investing: What Active Institutional Investors Want From Management*.

[179] Russell Reynolds Associates, *Redefining Corporate Governance*.

[180] *Research Question #1* : Are institutional owners actively involved in the strategic affairs of companies in their portfolios?

[181] Romano, "Public Pension Fund Activism."

[182] *Research Question #3* : When institutional owners are actively involved, which forms of institutional activism are most effective?

[183] *Research Question #4* : Does the type of institution affect its pursuit of shareholder activism?

[184] Carleton, Nelson and Weisbach, "The Influence of TIAA-CREF on Corporate Governance." Schultz and Warren, "Big Victory for Institutional Investors."

[185] Daily, Johnson, Ellstrand, and Dalton, *Institutional Investor Activism: Follow the Leaders?*

[186] Nesbitt, "Long-term Rewards from Shareholder Activism: a Study of the "CalPERS Effect." Opler and Sokobin, *Does Coordinated Institutional Activism Work? An Analysis of the Activities of the Council of Institutional Investors.*

[187] CalSTERS, *1996 Annual Comprehensive Financial Report of the California State Teachers' Retirement System*, (Sacramento, CA: CalSTERS, 1996).

[188] Brickley, Lease, and Smith, "Ownership Structure." Hoskisson, Hitt, Johnson, and Grossman, "*Conflicting Voices: The Effects of Ownership Heterogeneity and Internal Governance on Corporate Strategy.* Sherman, Beldona, and Joshi, *Institutional Investors: Four distinctive types.*

[189] Useem, *Investor Capitalism.*

[190] Black, "Agents Watching Agents."

[191] Brickley, Lease, and Smith, "Ownership Structure."

[192] William Taylor, "Can Big Owners Make a Big Difference?" *Harvard Business Review* 68, No. 5 (1990): 70-82.

[193] Coffee, "The SEC and the Institutional Investor." Rock, "The Logic and (Uncertain) Significance of Institutional Shareholder Activism."

Appendix

THE CHANGING FACE OF CORPORATE OWNERSHIP: DO INSTITUTIONAL OWNERS AFFECT FIRM PERFORMANCE?

Dear Institutional Owner / Investor:

Institutional investors are changing the basic governance structure of corporations. In the last decade many institutional investors have become shareholder activists in the hope of improving the performance of individual firms in their portfolios.

I am trying to learn more about the role of institutional investors in US corporate governance. In this study, I am investigating the extent to which institutions practice shareholder activism and relational investing. I am trying to determine the policies and philosophies which underlie these activities, and the effects of these practices upon corporations.

For the purposes of my study, institutional owners/investors include public pension plans, private pension plans, mutual funds, insurance companies, bank trusts, and foundations and endowments. Your organization was randomly selected from lists of these types of organizations in order to investigate the breadth of institutional shareholder activism and relational investing.

The questions which follow address your organization's ownership philosophy and policies, your use of your ownership position to affect firms in your investment portfolio, and the effects of your actions, if you take any, on your portfolio's returns. Due to your management philosophies and policies, and the extent of your activism, not all questions may apply to your institution.

Would you please complete the survey which follows in this booklet and return it to me in the self-addressed, stamped envelope. Your response will be kept confidential and your answers will be combined and analyzed with those of all other respondents.

I would like to supplement my understanding of your organization's ownership actions with any other information which you would provide me. If your organization issues a report of its performance, would you please forward a copy to me. Similarly, I would appreciate copies of any written investment and/or voting objectives or guidelines of your organization.

In advance, I want to thank you for your participation. Completing this project would not be possible without your help.

Sincerely yours,

Michael J. Rubach, J.D

General Directions: Please fill in the appropriate response or place an "x" next to the appropriate response for each question.

PART 1: SHAREHOLDER ACTIVISM

1. Description of General Investment Policy:

Before answering this question, please consider the following statements describing a firm's investment policy and activities and the way of selecting specific investments in your industry. After reading both descriptions, please select the one which most closely describes your fund's investment policy at the present time. Although neither statement may be exact, choose the one that most closely describes your institution's investment policy [Check only one blank]:

_____ 1. We invest to maximize direct financial wealth. The purpose of the fund is to maximize the benefits to the owners and beneficiaries. Benefits are defined in solely financial terms and are expressed as a percentage return on capital. We are expected to invest as an ordinary reasonably prudent investor, taking into consideration a variety of factors such as risk, diversification, and financial returns. Our investment activities are performed for the sole benefit of our owners and beneficiaries.

_____ 2 Instead of investing for maximum financial wealth, we invest for optimal returns. The purpose of the fund is to optimize the benefits for all of the fund's constituents. This requires balancing the multiple and specific interests of the owners and beneficiaries of our funds, employees of the firms in which we invest, the communities in which we are located and society as a whole. While striving to achieve real economic growth over the long term, optimal returns are defined by both financial and non-financial economic returns. Our investment activities are performed for the benefit of our multiple constituents, just not owners and beneficiaries.

2. **Voting of Proxies:** The following questions address the issue of who votes the proxies for shares in your portfolio—whether it is done internally or by external fund managers.

   2a. Are the shares within your portfolio voted by external fund managers?
   NO _____ YES _____

[if YES, answer questions 2b - 2d.; If NO, skip to question #3 on page 4.]

2b. What percentage of the shares in your portfolio are voted by external fund managers?

None	Some	One-half	Most	Entirely
1	2	3	4	5

2c. Does your fund establish and maintain a written policy for voting the shares which you own?

NO _____   YES _____

2d. If the answer to 2c is YES , does this written policy apply to your external fund managers?

NO _____   YES _____

[if YES, answer questions # 2e-2k; on the next page ; if NO, skip to question #3 on page 4.]

With respect to your written policy for voting share proxies, for each of the following issues, **Circle 'Y' for Yes or 'N' for No.**

'Policy' =   Do you have a Policy for Voting on this Issue?

'Management' =   Do you have a policy of voting with management on this issue?

Understand' =   Do your External Fund managers understand this policy?

'Discuss' =   Do you discuss with the External Fund Managers how they should vote on this issue?

'Monitor' =   Do you monitor the voting of the External Fund Managers on this issue?

	Policy	Management	Understand	Discuss	Monitor
2e. Votes for Control of the Corporation	Y N	Y N	Y N	Y N	Y N
2e(1). Poison Pills	Y N	Y N	Y N	Y N	Y N
2f. Mergers and Acquisitions	Y N	Y N	Y N	Y N	Y N
2g. Shareholder Corporate Governance Proposals	Y N	Y N	Y N	Y N	Y N
2g(1). Cumulative Voting	Y N	Y N	Y N	Y N	Y N
2h. Shareholder Social Issue Proposals	Y N	Y N	Y N	Y N	Y N

	Policy	Management	Understand	Discuss	Monitor
2i. Board of Directors' Elections	Y N	Y N	Y N	Y N	Y N
2j. Management Compensation	Y N	Y N	Y N	Y N	Y N
2j(1). Golden Parachutes	Y N	Y N	Y N	Y N	Y N
2j(2). Stock Options	Y N	Y N	Y N	Y N	Y N
2k. Director Compensation	Y N	Y N	Y N	Y N	Y N
2k(1). Stock Ownership	Y N	Y N	Y N	Y N	Y N
2k(2). Stock Options	Y N	Y N	Y N	Y N	Y N
2k(3). Pension Benefits	Y N	Y N	Y N	Y N	Y N

3. **Shareholder Activism.** The following questions address your activities with respect to shareholder activism. If your portfolio is externally managed or if your firm does not practice shareholder activism (i.e., participation in proxy contests, shareholder derivative suits, shareholder sponsored proposals, "Just Vote No" campaigns, and the issuance of hit lists of under performers), skip to question #4 on page 6; otherwise please answer the questions with respect to your shareholder activism performed **during your last fund /plan year**.

ACTIVITY	FREQUENCY PERFORMED				
	NEVER	RARELY	SOME-TIMES	OFTEN	VERY OFTEN
a. Initiated a proxy contest for control of a company ("proxy contest")	1	2	3	4	5
b. Voted with the proponent of a proxy contest.	1	2	3	4	5
c. Contacted other institutional investors to influence how they would vote in a proxy contest.	1	2	3	4	5
d. Been contacted by other institutional investors to influence how you voted in a proxy contest.	1	2	3	4	5

ACTIVITY	FREQUENCY PERFORMED				
	NEVER	RARELY	SOME-TIMES	OFTEN	VERY OFTEN
e. Filed a shareholder derivative suit or a shareholder class action suit ("shareholder suit")	1	2	3	4	5
f. Became a party to a shareholder suit as a plaintiff.	1	2	3	4	5
g. Supplied funds or services in support of a shareholder suit.	1	2	3	4	5
h. Contacted other institutional investor(s) with regard to becoming a party in a share-holder suit.	1	2	3	4	5
i. Been contacted by another institutional investor with regard to becoming a party to a shareholder suit.	1	2	3	4	5
j. Contacted other institutional investors with regard to supply-ing funds or services to support a shareholder suit.	1	2	3	4	5
k. Been contacted by another institutional investor with regard to supplying funds or ser-vices to support a share-holder suit.	1	2	3	4	5
l. Filed a shareholder sponsored proposal.	1	2	3	4	5

ACTIVITY	FREQUENCY PERFORMED				
	NEVER	RARELY	SOME-TIMES	OFTEN	VERY OFTEN
m. Became a sponsor for a shareholder proposal.	1	2	3	4	5
n. Contacted other institutional investor(s) with regard to sponsoring a shareholder proposal.	1	2	3	4	5
o. Been contacted by another institutional investor with regard to sponsoring a shareholder proposal.	1	2	3	4	5
p. Voted for a shareholder proposal.	1	2	3	4	5
q. Contacted other institutional investor(s) with regard to voting for a shareholder sponsored proposal.	1	2	3	4	5
r. Been contacted by another institutional investor with regard to voting for a shareholder sponsored proposal.	1	2	3	4	5
s. Initiated/sponsored a "Just Vote No" campaign.	1	2	3	4	5
t. Became a co-sponsor of a "just Vote No" campaign.	1	2	3	4	5
u. Contacted other institution investor(s) with regard to sponsoring "Just Vote No" Campaign.	1	2	3	4	5

| ACTIVITY | FREQUENCY PERFORMED | | | | |
	NEVER	RARELY	SOME-TIMES	OFTEN	VERY OFTEN
v. Been contacted by another institution with regard to sponsoring a "Just Vote No" Campaign.	1	2	3	4	5
w. Voted in support of a "Just Vote No" Campaign	1	2	3	4	5
x. Contacted other institutional investor(s) with regard to voting in support of a "Just Vote No" Campaign.	1	2	3	4	5
y. Been contacted by another institutional investor with regard to voting in support of a "Just Vote No" campaign.	1	2	3	4	5
z. Prepared a list of underperforming firms in your portfolio.	1	2	3	4	5
aa. Prepared a list of underperforming directors of companies in your portfolio.	1	2	3	4	5
bb. Disclosed any of the lists of underperforming companies or directors to the public.	1	2	3	4	5
cc. Sold shares of stock in an attempt to influence the corporate governance of a company.	1	2	3	4	5

ACTIVITY	FREQUENCY PERFORMED				
	NEVER	RARELY	SOME-TIMES	OFTEN	VERY OFTEN
dd. Sold shares of stock to influence the business strategy of a company.	1	2	3	4	5

4. Relational Investing: The following questions relate to a concept called "Relational Investing." Relational investing generally comprises your interactions with members of boards of directors and top management teams of the companies in your portfolio, and with other institutional owners/investors.

4a. INTERACTIONS with **BOARD MEMBERS** (excluding the CEO and other employee directors):

YES, # of Contacts per
Week Month Year

Personal Contact(s) (Face to Face):

Formal Business Meetings (regularly
scheduled and planned)   NO YES ____ ____ ____

Securities Analysts' Meetings
(Informational Meetings
set up by securities analysts)   NO YES ____ ____ ____

Informal Business Meetings
(irregular and unplanned)   NO YES ____ ____ ____

Formal Social Contacts (regularly
scheduled and planned)   NO YES ____ ____ ____

Informal Social Contacts
(irregular and unplanned)   NO YES ____ ____ ____

Oral Contact(s):

Formal telephone conversations
(regularly scheduled and planned)   NO YES ____ ____ ____

Informal telephone conversations
(irregular and unplanned)   NO YES ____ ____ ____

	YES, # of Contacts per
	Week Month Year

Written Contact(s):

Correspondence	NO YES ____ ____ ____
Reports	NO YES ____ ____ ____
E-Mail	NO YES ____ ____ ____

Topics Actually Discussed with Board Members
[Check all that apply]:

____ Financial Performance of the Firm	____ Prospects for Growth of Firm
____ Advertising and Promotion of Products	____ Employment Practices
____ CEO/Top Management Team Performance	____ Prospects for Growth of Industry
____ Competitors	____ Customer/Supplier Relationships
____ Top management team Succession	____ Product Pricing
____ Stock Performance	____ Business Strategy
____ Corporate Governance Issues	____ Research and Development Expenditures

4b. Have you attempted to contact a board member of a firm in your portfolio and been refused
NO _____   YES _____   If YES, How many times _____

4c. INTERACTIONS with **TOP MANAGEMENT TEAM MEMBERS** (including the CEO and employees who are board members):

| | YES, # of Contacts per | | |
| | Week | Month | Year |

Personal Contact(s) (Face to Face):

Formal Business Meetings (regularly scheduled and planned)	NO	YES ____	____	____
Securities Analysts' Meetings (Informational Meetings set up by security analysts)	NO	YES ____	____	____
Informal Business Meetings (irregular and unplanned)	NO	YES ____	____	____
Formal Social Contacts (regularly scheduled and planned)	NO	YES ____	____	____
Informal Social Contacts (irregular and unplanned)	NO	YES ____	____	____

Oral Contact(s):

Formal telephone conversations (regularly scheduled and planned)	NO	YES ____	____	____
Informal telephone conversations (irregular and unplanned)	NO	YES ____	____	____

Written Contact(s):

Correspondence	NO	YES ____	____	____
Reports	NO	YES ____	____	____
E-Mail	NO	YES ____	____	____

Topics Actually Discussed with Top Management Team Members
[Check all that apply]:

____ Financial Performance of the Firm   ____ Prospects for Growth of Firm

____ Advertising and Promotion of Products   ____ Employment Practices

____ CEO/Top Management Team Performance   ____ Prospects for Growth of Industry

____ Competitors   ____ Customer/Supplier
                                         Relationships

____ Top management team   ____ Product Pricing
     Succession

____ Stock Performance   ____ Business Strategy

____ Corporate Governance Issues   ____ Research and Development
                                         Expenditures

4d. INTERACTIONS with **OTHER INSTITUTIONAL INVESTORS:**

		YES, # of Contacts per		
		Week	Month	Year
Personal Contact(s) (Face to Face):				
Formal Business Meetings (regularly scheduled and planned)	NO YES	____	____	____
Securities Analysts' Meetings (Informational Meetings set up by security analysts)	NO YES	____	____	____
Informal Business Meetings (irregular and unplanned)	NO YES	____	____	____
Formal Social Contacts (regularly scheduled and planned)	NO YES	____	____	____
Informal Social Contacts (irregular and unplanned)	NO YES	____	____	____
Oral Contact(s):				
Formal telephone conversations (regularly scheduled and planned)	NO YES	____	____	____
Informal telephone conversations (irregular and unplanned)	NO YES	____	____	____
Written Contact(s):				
Correspondence	NO YES	____	____	____
Reports	NO YES	____	____	____
E-Mail	NO YES	____	____	____

Topics Actually Discussed with Other Institutional Investors [Check all that apply]:

____ Financial Performance of the Firm	____ Prospects for Growth of Firm
____ Advertising and Promotion of Products	____ Employment Practices
____ CEO/Top Management Team Performance	____ Prospects for Growth of Industry
____ Competitors	____ Customer/Supplier Relationships
____ Top management team Succession	____ Product Pricing
____ Stock Performance	____ Business Strategy
____ Corporate Governance Issues	____ Research and Development Expenditures

5. Affiliations:

5a Do any of your board members sit on the boards of other organizations [Check all that apply]:

____ For-profit companies in which you invest.
____ For-profit companies which are not part of your investments.
____ Not-for -Profit Organizations located in the area where you are headquartered.
____ Not-for-Profit Organizations located in areas where you have facilities or offices.
____ Boards which represent Beneficiaries of your investments.
____ Other institutional owners/investors.
____ Governmental agencies.

5b. Is your institution a member of any institutional trade organization or service organization?

        YES ____   NO ____

5c. If the answer to Question 5b is YES, please check all that apply:
____ Council of Institutional Investors
____ Other [please list].

_____

_____

PART 2: GENERAL INFORMATION & INVESTMENT RETURNS

Directions: The following questions address the investment policy and investment returns of your fund. Please fill in the appropriate response or place an "x" next to the appropriate response for each question

6. Year your organization/plan/fund was created: _____

7. Size of your total fund assets ?

Book Value $_____   Market Value $_____

8. For your current year:

Annual rate of return on total assets?   _____ <5%
_____ 5<x<10%
_____ 10<x<15%
_____ 15<x<20%
_____ >20%

Asset Allocation Percentage for Equities?

	Actual or Targeted Allocation (%)[1]	Managed Internally (%)[2]
Equities:		
Domestic:	_____	_____
International:	_____	_____

8b. For Fund Year 1996:

Return on Total Assets?   _____ <5%
_____ 5<x<10%
_____ 10<x<15%
_____ 15<x<20%
_____ >20%

Asset Allocation Percentage for Equities?

	Actual or Targeted Allocation (%)[1]	Managed Internally (%)[2]
Equities:		
Domestic:	_____	_____
International:	_____	_____

8c. For Fund Year 1995:

Return on Total Assets?
_____ <5%
_____ 5<x<10%
_____ 10<x<15%
_____ 15<x<20%
_____ >20%

Asset Allocation Percentage for Equities?

	Actual or Targeted Allocation (%)[1]	Managed Internally (%)[2]
Equities:		
Domestic:	_____	_____
International:	_____	_____

[1] These numbers should reflect the percentage of your total assets which comprise equities; the column's total may not equal 100%, unless all of you assets are invested in equities. You may use either actual or targeted allocation of equities, which ever is easier

[2] The columns should reflect the percentage of the equities which you manage internally, not utilizing external fund managers; the column's total may not equal 100%.

9. What is the size of your administrative board? _____ (#)

10. Is your board appointed? YES _____ NO _____

10a. If YES, By whom?
_____
_____

11. Is your board elected? YES _____ NO _____

11. If YES, By whom?
_____
_____

12. What is the size of your administrative staff?   _____ (#)

13. What is the size of your administrative budget?   _____($)

14. How often does your asset allocation change? [Select number which most clearly reflects how often your allocation is changed]:

Never	Rarely	Occasionally	Fairly Often	Very Often
1	2	3	4	5

15. Who sets your asset allocation? [Check all that apply]:

_____ Board/Trustees   _____ Investment officers
_____ Investment Counsel/Consultants   _____ Other _____

16. Describe your investment philosophy with regards to investments in individual companies? [Select number which best characterizes your investment philosophy]:

Buy and   Trade Shares Often to
Hold   Maximize Share Value
1   2   3   4   5

17. In your current calendar year, how often has your portfolio turned over? _____ [e.g., 1.5 times].

18. Under what investment restrictions do you operate? [Check all that apply]:

_____ Prudent Person Rule
_____ Federal Government Restrictions
_____ State Government Restrictions
_____ Other _____
_____ None

19. Does your fund establish and maintain written internal policy objectives and investment guidelines?
           YES _____   NO _____

20. There are various standards which can be used as guidelines for investments and investment opportunities. Using the following scale, please rate the importance of the standards set forth below.

Circle **1** if you believe that the standards are of equal importance
Circle **3** if you believe one standard is slightly more important than the other
Circle **5** if you believe one standard is somewhat more important

Circle **7** if you believe one standard is substantially more important
Circle **9** if you believe one standard totally dominates the other in importance.

Maximize Investment Returns	Diversify Fund Investments
9 7 5 3 1	3 5 7 9

Maximize Investment Returns	Preservation of Fund Principal
9 7 5 3 1	3 5 7 9

Maximize Investment Returns	Reduce Risk
9 7 5 3 1	3 5 7 9

Maximize Investment Returns	Consider Non-financial Returns
9 7 5 3 1	3 5 7 9

Maximize Investment Returns	Consider Effects on Multiple Constituents
9 7 5 3 1	3 5 7 9

Diversify Fund Investments	Preservation of Fund Principle
9 7 5 3 1	3 5 7 9

Diversify Fund Investments	Reduce Risk
9 7 5 3 1	3 5 7 9

Diversify Fund Investments	Consider Non-financial Returns
9 7 5 3 1	3 5 7 9

Diversify Fund Investments	Consider Effects on Multiple Constituents
9 7 5 3 1	3 5 7 9

Preservation of Fund Principal	Consider Non-financial Returns
9 7 5 3 1	3 5 7 9

Preservation of Fund Principal	Consider Effects on Multiple Constituents
9 7 5 3 1	3 5 7 9

Consider Non-financial Returns	Consider Effects on Multiple Constituents
9 7 5 3 1	3 5 7 9

If you believe there are other standards of equal or greater importance that should be included in your screening criteria you can specify them in the comments section on the last page of the booklet.

21. If a company in your portfolio is not meeting your policy objectives or investment guidelines, which of the following best describes what action you will take with regard to that company? [Select number which best characterizes your action]:

Hold the Entire Interest		Sell Part/ Hold Part		Sell All of the Interest
1	2	3	4	5

22. Do you utilize external fund managers?

    YES _____   [If YES, answer questions # 22a - 22c]
    NO _____   [If NO, skip to #23]

22a. How many external fund managers are you presently using? _____

22b. How would you describe your involvement in selecting or monitoring the stocks in an external fund manager's portfolio?

Never	Rare	Occasional	Frequent	Constant
1	2	3	4	5

22c. How often do you independently review investment selections of external fund managers?

Annually	Semi-Annually	Quarterly	Monthly	More Frequently
1	2	3	4	5

23. Do you utilize investment consultants and advisors to assist you in your investment decisions?

    YES _____   [If YES, answer questions # 23a–23c]
    NO _____   [If NO, skip to #24]

23a. How many investment consultants and advisors are you presently using? _____

23b. How would you describe your involvement in selecting or monitoring the stocks which the investment counselors or advisors recommend?

Never	Rare	Occasional	Frequent	Constant
1	2	3	4	5

23c. How often do you independently review the investment selections or advice of the investment counselors or advisors?

Annually	Semi-Annually	Quarterly	Monthly	More Frequently
1	2	3	4	5

24. Do you use indexing?

        YES _____   [If YES, answer questions # 24a–24d]

        NO _____   [If NO, skip to #25]

24a. What percentage of your fund is indexed? _____ [Indicate percentage use].

24b. How often do you screen/monitor your indexed funds (e.g., screen the funds for poor performers)?

Annually	Semi-Annually	Quarterly	Monthly	More Frequently
1	2	3	4	5

24c. If you screen/monitor all or part of your indexed funds, there are various criteria which can be used to evaluate investments. Using the following scale, please rate the importance of the investment criteria set forth below.

Circle **1** if you believe that the standards are of equal importance

Circle **3** if you believe one standard is slightly more important than the other

Circle **5** if you believe one standard is somewhat more important

Circle **7** if you believe one standard is substantially more important

Circle **9** if you believe one standard totally dominates the other in importance.

Financial Performance					Prospects for Growth			
9	7	5	3	1	3	5	7	9

Financial Performance					Quality of CEO/Top Management Team			
9	7	5	3	1	3	5	7	9

Financial Performance					Business Strategy			
9	7	5	3	1	3	5	7	9

Financial Performance					Stock Performance			
9	7	5	3	1	3	5	7	9

Financial Performance					Type of Industry			
9	7	5	3	1	3	5	7	9

Financial Performance					Quality of Corporate Governance			
9	7	5	3	1	3	5	7	9

Prospects for Growth					Quality of CEO/Top Management Team			
9	7	5	3	1	3	5	7	9

Prospects for Growth					Business Strategy			
9	7	5	3	1	3	5	7	9

Prospects for Growth					Stock Performance			
9	7	5	3	1	3	5	7	9

Prospects for Growth					Type of Industry			
9	7	5	3	1	3	5	7	9

Prospects for Growth					Quality of Corporate Governance			
9	7	5	3	1	3	5	7	9

Quality of CEO/Top Management Team					Business Strategy			
9	7	5	3	1	3	5	7	9

Quality of CEO/Top Management Team					Stock Performance			
9	7	5	3	1	3	5	7	9

Quality of CEO/Top Management Team					Type of Industry			
9	7	5	3	1	3	5	7	9

Quality of CEO/Top Management Team					Quality of Corporate Governance			
9	7	5	3	1	3	5	7	9

Business Strategy					Stock Performance			
9	7	5	3	1	3	5	7	9

Business Strategy					Type of Industry			
9	7	5	3	1	3	5	7	9

Business Strategy					Quality of Corporate Governance			
9	7	5	3	1	3	5	7	9

Stock performance					Type of Industry			
9	7	5	3	1	3	5	7	9

Stock Performance					Quality of Corporate Governance			
9	7	5	3	1	3	5	7	9

Type of Industry					Quality of Corporate Governance			
9	7	5	3	1	3	5	7	9

If you believe there are other categories of equal or greater importance that should be included in your screening criteria you can specify them in the comments section on the last page of the booklet.

24d. If a company in your indexed portfolio is not meeting your policy objectives or investment guidelines, which of the following best describes the action you will take. [Select number which best characterizes your philosophy]:

Continue to Hold the Interest Indefinitely				Sell the Interest Immediately
1	2	3	4	5

25. Specific Types of Investments.

The following questions address whether you target investments in real estate, municipal bonds, initial public offerings, capital ventures and/or newer ventures toward specific localities. Please indicate the location of the targeted investments in your portfolio. **Please circle as many as apply**. For each of the following:

1 = Metropolitan area or political subdivisions within the metropolitan area where you are headquartered ['M']
2 = State in which you are headquartered ['S']
3 = States in which you have facilities/offices ['F/O']
4 = United States ['US']
5 = Foreign countries ['F']
6 = Do not invest in this type of investment ['NOT']

	M	S	F/O	US	F	NOT
25a. Real estate or in investments which invest in real-estate (i.e., REITs , ltd. partnerships) [location of real estate]?	1	2	3	4	5	6
25b. Municipal Bonds [location of issuers]?	1	2	3	4	5	6
25c. Initial Public Offerings [location of issuers]?	1	2	3	4	5	6
25d. Capital Ventures (i.e. firms which are not publicly traded)?	1	2	3	4	5	6
25e. Newer Ventures? (i.e. firms which are new firms, less than eight [8] years old) ?	1	2	3	4	5	6

THANK YOU FOR COMPLETING THE SURVEY: PLEASE FEEL FREE TO USE THE BACK COVER TO PROVIDE ADDITIONAL COMMENTS ON THE ROLE OF INSTITUTIONAL INVESTORS IN CORPORATE GOVERNANCE AND INSTITUTIONAL SHAREHOLDER ACTIVISM.

COMMENTS:

Appendix B
LIST OF INSTITUTIONAL INVESTORS FOR FIRST SURVEY

PUBLIC PENSION PLANS:
ABILENE FIREMEN'S RELIEF
    RETIREMENT SYSTEM (R.S.)
ADAMS COUNTY RETIREMENT
    PLAN
ALBANY EMPLOYEES' PENSION
    FUND
ALEMEDA-CONTRA COSTA
    EMPLOYEES' RETIREMENT
    ASSOCIATION
AMES UTILITIES EMPLOYEES
    RETIREMENT FUND
ARKANSAS STATE HIGHWAY
    EMPLOYEES R.S.
ARKANSAS TEACHER R.S.
ATLANTA PENSION FUNDS
BALTIMORE R.S.
BARNSTABLE COUNTY R.S.
CALIFORNIA STATE TEACHERS R.S.
CHARLOTTE FIREFIGHTERS' R.S.
CHICAGO LABORERS' ANNUITY &
    BENEFIT FUND
CITY OF JACKSONVILLE
CITY OF MACON
CITY OF PITTSBURGH COMPREHEN-
    SIVE MUNICIPAL FUND
CITY OF STAMFORD
CITY OF TITUSVILLE
CITY OF WARWICK R.S.
COLORADO FIRE & POLICE PENSION
    ASSOC.
COLORADO COUNTY EMPLOYEES'
    RETIREMENT ASSOCIATION
DALLAS AREA RAPID TRANSIT
DALLAS EMPLOYEES' RETIREMENT
    FUND
DARIEN POLICE PENSION SYSTEM
DELAWARE COUNTY EMPLOYEES'
    R.S.
DENVER EMPLOYEES' RETIREMENT
    FUND
DETROIT POLICE & FIRE R.S.
EAST PROVIDENCE POLICE & FIRE
    R.S.
EAST HARTFORD TOWN R.S.

EL PASO CITY EMPLOYEES'
    RETIREMENT FUND
FAIRFAX COUNTY RETIREMENT
    FUNDS
FAIRFAX COUNTRY WATER
    AUTHORITY R.S.
FALL RIVER CONTRIBUTORY R.S.
FLORIDA STATE TREASURY
FRANKLIN COUNTY EMPLOYEES'
    RETIREMENT FUND
FRESNO COUNTY EMPLOYEES
    RETIREMENT ASSOCIATION
GENESEE COUNTY EMPLOYEES' R.S.
GLOUCESTER CONTRIBUTORY R.S.
HAMDEN TOWN PENSION SYSTEM
HASTINGS POLICE & FIREMEN'S
    PENSION FUND
HAWAII EMPLOYEES R.S.
HOLYOKE R.S.
HOUSTON POLICE OFFICERS'
    PENSION SYSTEM
ILLINOIS MUNICIPAL RETIREMENT
    FUND
ILLINOIS TEACHERS R.S.
JACKSONVILLE FIRE & POLICE
    PENSION FUND
KALAMAZOO COUNTY
    EMPLOYEES' R.S.
KANSAS CITY PUBLIC SCHOOL R.S.
KANSAS PUBLIC EMPLOYEES R.S.
KERN COUNTY EMPLOYEES
    RETIREMENT ASSOCIATION
LAKELAND FIREMEN'S PENSION
    FUND
LANSING BOARD OF WATER &
    LIGHT
LEHIGH COUNTY EMPLOYEES'
    RETIREMENT FUND
LOMBARD POLICE & FIREMEN'S
    PENSION FUNDS
LOS ANGELES CERA
LOS ANGELES WATER & POWER
    EMPLOYEES R.S.
LOUISIANA SCHOOL EMPLOYEES
    R.S.

LOUISIANA STATE POLICE
R.S.
MAINE STATE R.S.
MARICOPA COUNTY
MARION COUNTY LAW
ENFORCEMENT TRUST
MARYLAND TEACHERS ...
SUPPLEMENTAL
RETIREMENT PLANS
MASSACHUSETTS PENSIONS
RESERVE INVEST.
MANAGEMENT BOARD
MEMPHIS LIGHT, GAS & WATER
DIVISION PENSION SYSTEM
MENDOCINO COUNTY EMPLOYEES'
RETIREMENT ASSOCIATION
MFPRS OF IOWA
MIAMI BEACH R.S. FOR GENERAL
EMPLOYEES
MICHIGAN DEPARTMENT OF
TREASURY
MIDLAND FIREMEN'S RELIEF &
RETIREMENT TRUST
MILWAUKEE EMPLOYEES R.S.
MISSISSIPPI PUBLIC EMPLOYEES
R.S.
MONMOUTH POLICE & FIREMEN'S
PENSION FUNDS
MONROE EMPLOYEES' R.S.
MONTANA BOARD OF
INVESTMENTS
MONTGOMERY COUNTY
RETIREMENT BOARD
MUNICIPAL EMPLOYEES' R.S. OF
LOUISIANA
NASHUA BOARD OF PUBLIC WORKS
EMPLOYEES' R.S.
NEVADA PUBLIC EMPLOYEES R.S.
NEW MEXICO EDUCATIONAL
RETIREMENT BOARD
NEW ORLEANS FIREMEN'S R.S.
NEW ORLEANS SEWERAGE &
WATER BOARD .PENSION
PLAN
NEW YORK CITY TEACHERS
VARIABLE FUND
NEW YORK STATE TEACHERS R.S.
NORFOLK EMPLOYEES' R.S.

NORTHAMPTON CONTRIBUTORY
R.S.
OHIO POLICE & FIREMEN'S
DISABILITY & PENSION
BOARD
OHIO SCHOOL EMPLOYEES' R.S.
OKLAHOMA COUNTY EMPLOYEES'
R.S.
OKLAHOMA LAW ENFORCEMENT
R.S.
OKLAHOMA TEACHERS' R.S.
OMAHA SCHOOL EMPLOYEES' R.S.
OWOSSO R.S.
PENNSYLVANIA PUBLIC SCHOOL
EMPLOYEES' R.S.
PHOENIX CITY EMPLOYEES' R.S.
PONCA CITY RETIREMENT BOARD
PORT ARTHUR FIREMEN'S RELIEF
RETIREMENT FUND
PRINCE GEORGES COUNTY
PUBLIC SCHOOL TEACHERS'
PENSION FUND OF CHICAGO
PUBLIC SCHOOL R.S. OF MISSOURI
RETIREMENT BOARD OF
ALLEGHENY COUNTY
ROCK ISLAND POLICE & FIRE
PENSION SYSTEM
ROCKFORD FIREMEN'S & POLICE
PENSION FUNDS
ST. CLAIR SHORES EMPLOYEES' R.S.
ST. LOUIS POLICE R.S.
ST. LOUIS PUBLIC SCHOOL R.S.
SAN DIEGO CITY EMPLOYEES' R.S.
SAN FRANCISCO CITY & COUNTY
EMPLOYEES' R.S.
SEATTLE CITY EMPLOYEES R.S.
SHELBY COUNTY R.S.
SKOKIE FIRE & POLICE PENSION
FUNDS
STATE OF CONNECTICUT TRUST
FUNDS
STRATFORD TOWN EMPLOYEES'
PENSION PLAN
TAMPA POLICE & FIREFIGHTERS'
PENSION FUND
TAYLOR POLICE & FIRE R.S.
TENNESSEE CONSOLIDATED R.S.
TEXAS MUNICIPAL R.S.

TOWN OF GREENWICH R.S.
TOWNSHIP OF SHALER ... POLICE
    PENSION PLANS
UNIVERSITY OF CALIFORNIA
VIRGINIA R.S.
WASHINGTON COUNTY
    EMPLOYEES' R.S.
WEST VIRGINIA CONSOLIDATED
    PUBLIC RETIREMENT BOARD
WESTMINSTER FIREMEN'S PENSION
    FUND
WINCHESTER BOARD OF
    RETIREMENT
WINSTON SALEM EMPLOYEES' R.S.
WISCONSIN INVESTMENT BOARD

PRIVATE PENSION PLANS::

A N R FREIGHT SYSTEMS
ABRIDGE WIRE CLOTH CO.
ADVO, INC.
ALDI, INC.
AMER. CUNNINGHAM & BRENNAN
    CO.
AMERICAN INTERNATIONAL GROUP
AMERICAN COUNCIL LIFE INS.
    ASSOCIATION
AMERITECH
ANHEUSER BUSCH CO, INC.
ARATEX SERVICES, INC.
ATLANTIC MARINE, INC.
BACARDI IMPORTS, INC.
BALL CORP
BARCLAYS BANK, PLC.
BECKWITH MACHINERY CO.
BEN ARNOLD CO., INC.
BEST CUTTING DIE CO.
BLOOMER CHOCOLATE CO.
BOEING CO
BOICE WILLIS CLINIC
BRAUM ICE CREAM STORES, INC.
BROWN PRINTING CO
BRUSH WELLMAN, INC.
BUTLER MACHINERY CO.
CARSON PIRIE SCOTT & CO.
CASCADE NATURAL GAS CORP.
CENTRAL STATES DIVERSIFIED, INC.
CERIDIAN CORP
CHESAPEAKE UTILITIES CORP.

CITY MILL CO., LTD.
COHERENT MANAGEMENT
    SYSTEMS
CONAGRA, INC
CONSOLIDATED FREIGHTWAYS, INC
COORS BREWING CO
CSZ CORP
CUMMINS ENGINE CO, INC
CURRENT, INC.
DANA CORP.
DELMARVA POWER & LIGHT CO
DELOITTE & TOUCHE
DIGITAL ELECTRONIC AUTO. INC.
DOVER DIVERSIFIED
DSST SYSTEMS, INC.
DYNAMICS RESEARCH CORP.
ELI LILLY & CO
ETHYL CORP
FAIRCHILD SPACE & DEFENSE CORP
THE FARM CREDIT BANK OF
    COLUMBIA
FEDERAL EXPRESS CORP.
FEDERATED DEPT STORES, INC
FIGGIE INTERNATIONAL, INC.
FIRST DATA CORP.
FIRST NH BANKS, INC.
FOREST OIL CORP.
FREEPORT MCMORAN, INC.
GENERAL MILLS INC
GEORGIA PACIFIC CORP
GREYHOUND LINES, INC.
H & R BLOCH, INC
H.E. BUTT GROCERY CO.
HALLMARK CARDS, INC.
HARTER SECREST & EMERY
HEALTHEAST
HEARST CORP
HITACHI AMERICA, LTD
HONEYWELL INC
HUGHES, HUBBARD & REED
IMO INDUSTRIES
INTERSTATE BRANDS CORP
IOWA ILLINOIS GAS & ELECTRIC CO.
ITT CORPORATION
JC PENNEY CO., INC
JOHN H. HARLAND CO.
KOCH INDUSTRIES, INC.
KOHLER CO.

KRISPY KREME DOUGHNUT CORP.
LARSON MANUFACTURING CO.,
    INC.
LEARJET, INC.
LENNOX INDUSTRIES, INC.
LIBBY OWENS FORD CO
LINCOLN TELEPHONE &
    TELEGRAPH
LINCOLN NATIONAL CORP
LONG ISLAND SAVINGS BANK
LONGS DRUG STORES CALIFORNIA,
    INC.
THE MARMON GROUP, INC.
MATSUSHITA ELEC CORP. OF
    AMERICA
MAYTAG CORP
MCJUNKIN CORP
MDU RESOURCES GROUP, INC.
MEAD CORPORATION
MEMPHIS HARDWOOD FLOORING
    CO.
MEREDITH CORP.
MIDWESTERN MACHINERY CO., INC.
MINNESOTA MINING &
    MANUFACTURING
NATIONAL BASKETBALL
    ASSOCIATION
NORTHERN STATES POWER CO
ORYX ENERGY COMPANY
OWENS CORNING FIBERGLASS
    CORP.
PACIFIC GAS & ELECTRIC CO
PACIFIC TELESIS CORP.
PICCADILLY CAFETERIAS, INC.
PICHIN CORP
THE PILLSBURY CO
RALSTON PURINA CO.
RAYCHEM CORP
ROCHESTER GAS & ELECTRIC CORP
RUSSELL CORPORATION
SAFEWAY, INC
SPRINT CORP
STAUFFER COMMUNICATIONS, INC.
STONECUTTER MILLS CORP.
SUN COAL CO.
US WEST, INC
UTILICORP UNITED, INC.
VIKING FREIGHT SYSTEM, INC.

THE WILLIAM CARTER CO.
THE WILLIAMS COMPANIES
W.W. GRAINGER, INC.
WHITE CONSOLIDATED
    INDUSTRIES, INC
THE WILLIAMS COMPANIES
W.W. GRAINGER, INC.

**PRIVATE PENSION PLANS / UNION
PLANS:**

ASBESTOS WORKERS, LOCAL #47,
    COLDWATER, MI
BAKERY, CONFECTIONARY &
    TOBACCO WORKERS,
    CLEVELAND, OH
BOILERMAKERS - BLACKSMITHS
    NATIONAL PENSION TRUST
BOILERMAKERS, LOCAL #5, GREAT
    NECK, NY
BRICK MASONS PENSION TRUST, EL
    MONTE, CA
CARPENTERS, LOCALS
    WASHINGTON & IDAHO,
    SPOKANE, WA
CARPENTERS, DISTRICT COUNCIL,
    MADISON, NJ
CARPENTERS, LOCAL #345,
    MEMPHIS, TN
CARPENTERS, OHIO PENSION FUND,
    CLEVELAND, OH
CARPENTERS, DISTRICT COUNCIL,
    SOUTH FLORIDA, HIALEAH,
    FL
DISTILLERY WORKERS, LOCAL #3,
    CHICAGO, IL
ELECTRIC WORKERS, IBEW LOCAL
    #861, LAKE CHARLES, LA
ELECTRIC WORKERS, IBEW #134,
    CHICAGO, IL
ELECTRICAL WORKERS, IUE,
    DISTRICT #3, EAST
    RUTHERFORD, NJ
ELECTRICAL WORKERS, IBEW #175,
    CHATTANOOGA, TN
ELECTRICAL WORKERS, IBEW #1,
    ST. LOUIS, MO
ELECTRICAL WORKERS, IBEW #358,
    PERTH AMBOY, NJ

ELECTRICAL WORKERS, IUE, LOCAL #475, PELHAM, NY

ENGINEERS, OPERATING LOCAL #542, NORRISTOWN, PA

F&CW LOCAL #576, KANSAS CITY, MO

F&CW, LOCAL #100, CHICAGO, IL

FURNITURE WORKERS, NATIONAL HEADQUARTERS, NASHVILLE, TN

GARMENT WORKERS, ILGWU, NY, NY

IAM NATIONAL PENSION FUND, WASHINGTON, DC

INDUSTRIAL TRADE UNIONS, NATIONAL ORGANIZATION

IRON WORKERS, DISTRICT COUNCIL, ST. LOUIS, MO

IRON WORKERS, LOCAL #625, WAIPALNU, HI

LABORERS, DETROIT VICINITY, BINGHAM FARMS, MI

LABORERS, LOCAL #157, SCHENECTADY, NY

LABORERS, SO. CALIFORNIA, CONTRACTING PLASTERERS ASSOC.

LABORERS LOCAL #731, NY, NY

LABORERS, CONSTRUCTION & GENERAL, WESTCHESTER, IL

LONGSHOREMAN LOCALS 1410, 1401-1, 1459,MOBILE, AL

LONGSHOREMAN, STA-ILA, PENSION TR, BALTIMORE, MD

MACHINISTS, LOCAL #698, DETROIT, MI

MARINE ENGINEERS (MEBA)

NATIONAL ELEVATOR INDUSTRY, NEWTON SQUARE, PA

NMU PENSION & WELFARE PLAN, NY, NY

OPERATING ENGINEERS PENSION TRUST, PASADENA, CA

PIPE TRADES, IDAHO TRUST, BOISE, ID

PLASTERERS & CEMENT MASONS BELLWOOD, IL

PLUMBERS & PIPEFITTERS, LOCAL #212,

PLUMBERS & PIPEFITTERS, LOCAL #537, BOSTON, MA

PLUMBERS, LOCAL #525, LAS VEGAS, NV

PLUMBERS, LOCAL #149, SAVOY, IL

PLUMBERS, LOCAL #690, PHILADELPHIA, PA

RETAIL CLERKS & EMPLOYERS, NO. CALIF., WALNUT CREEK, CA

ROOFERS, LOCAL #9, EAST HARTFORD, CT

SHEET METAL WORKERS, LOCAL #54, HOUSTON, TX

SHEET METAL WORKERS INTERNATIONAL, WASHINGTON, DC

SHEET METAL WORKERS, LOCAL #293, HONOLULU, HI

TEAMSTERS, LOCAL #2, BUTTE, MT

TEAMSTERS, LOCAL #753, CHICAGO, IL

TEAMSTERS, LOCAL #282, LAKE SUCCESS, NY

TEAMSTERS, WESTERN CONFERENCE, SEATTLE, WA

TEAMSTERS, LOCAL #456, ELMSFORD, NY

UFCW - INTERNATIONAL UNION, CHICAGO, IL

MUTUAL FUNDS / MONEY MANAGERS:

ACADIAN ASSET MANAGEMENT, INC.

ALLIANCE CAPITAL MANAGEMENT, LP

AMB INSTITUTIONAL REALTY ADVISORS

AMCORE TRUST COMPANY

ARIEL CAPITAL MANAGEMENT, INC.

ASB CAPITAL MANAGEMENT, INC.

B OF A CAPITAL MANAGEMENT, INC.

BANC ONE INVESTMENT ADVISORS CORP.

BARNETT BANKS TRUST COMPANY,
  NA
BARON CAPITAL MANAGEMENT,
  INC.
BARTLETT & CO.
BEA ASSOCIATES
BERGER ASSOCIATES
BILLARD, BIEHL & KAISER, INC.
BLACKROCK FINANCIAL
  MANAGEMENT, LP
BLAIRLOGIE CAPITAL
  MANAGEMENT LTD.
BOSTON INTERNATIONAL
  ADVISORS, INC.
BRINSON PARTNERS, INC.
BRUNDAGE, STORY & ROSE
CAPITAL RESEARCH &
  MANAGEMENT CO.
CAPITAL GROWTH MANAGEMENT
CIGNA RETIREMENT &
  INVESTMENT SERVICES
COLONIAL MANAGEMENT
  ASSOCIATES, INC.
COLUMBIA MANAGEMENT CO.
COLUMBUS CIRCLE INVESTORS
COMPOSITE RESEARCH &
  MANAGEMENT COMPANY
CORNERSTONE CAPITAL
  INVESTMENT COUNSEL
COWEN ASSET MANAGEMENT
THE CRABBE HUSON GROUP, INC
CS FIRST BOSTON INVESTMENT
  MANAGEMENT CORP.
CUTLER & COMPANY, INC.
DAVID COOK & ASSOCIATES, INC.
DAVID L. BABSON & CO.
DEAN WITTER INTERCAPITAL INC.
DELAWARE MANAGEMENT CO.
DENVER INVESTMENT ADVISORS
DODGE & COX, INC.
DREMAN VALUE MANAGEMENT, LP
THE DREYFUS CORPORATION
EATON VANCE MANAGEMENT
FIRST PACIFIC ADVISORS, INC.
FIRST INVESTORS MANAGEMENT
  COMPANY, INC.
FORTIS ADVISERS

FOUNDERS ASSET MANAGEMENT,
  INC.
FRANKLIN TEMPLETON/FRANKLIN
  ADVISERS, INC.
FRED ALGER MANAGEMENT, INC.
FREEDOM CAPITAL MANAGEMENT
  CORP.
FREMONT INVESTMENT ADVISORS,
  INC.
FRIESS ASSOCIATES, INC.
GABELLI-O'CONNOR FIXED
  INCOME MANAGEMENT CO.
GE INVESTMENT MANAGEMENT
  INC.
GLOBAL ASSET MANAGEMENT
  (USA), INC.
GREENWICH STREET ADVISORS
HAWTHORNE ASSOCIATES, INC.
HIGHLAND CAPITAL MANAGEMENT
  CORP.
HYPERION CAPITAL MANAGEMENT,
  INC.
IAA TRUST COMPANY
IDS ADVISORY GROUP, INC.
INVESCO TRUST CO.
INVESTMENT ADVISERS, INC.
INVESTORS RESEARCH CORP.
JAMES INVESTMENT RESEARCH,
  INC.
JANUS CAPITAL CORP.
JOHN HANCOCK ADVISERS
JULIUS BAER INVESTMENT
  MANAGEMENT, INC.
KEYSTONE GROUP, INC.
KPM INVESTMENT MANAGEMENT,
  INC.
LAZARD FRERES ASSET
  MANAGEMENT
LEGG MASON CAPITAL
  MANAGEMENT, INC.
LEHMAN BROTHERS GLOBAL ASSET
  MANAGEMENT
LEXINGTON MANAGEMENT CORP.
LIEBER & CO.
LINCOLN CAPITAL MANAGEMENT
  COMPANY
LIPPER & CO., LP
LOOMIS, SAYLES & COMPANY, L.P.

LORD, ABBETT & CO., INC.
M & I INVESTMENT MANAGEMENT
 CORP.
MELLON CAPITAL MANAGEMENT
 CORP.
MERIDIAN INVESTMENT COMPANY
MERRILL LYNCH ASSET
 MANAGEMENT
MFS-MASSACHUSETTS FINANCIAL
 SERVICES COMPANY
MISSISSIPPI VALLEY ADVISERS, INC.
MITCHELL HUTCHINS ASSET
 MANAGEMENT INC
MONTAG & CALDWELL, INC.
MONTGOMERY ASSET
 MANAGEMENT
MORGAN GRENFELL CAPITAL
 MANAGEMENT, INC.
MUNDER CAPITAL MANAGEMENT
NEUBERGER & BERMAN
NICHOLAS-APPLEGATE CAPITAL
 MANAGEMENT
NORTHWEST CAPITAL
 MANAGEMENT
OLD KENT BANK & TRUST
 COMPANY
OPPENHEIMER CAPITAL
PACIFIC INVESTMENT
 MANAGEMENT COMPANY
PANAGORA ASSET MANAGEMENT
PILGRIM BAXTER & ASSOCIATES
THE PILGRIM GROUP
PIONEERING MANAGEMENT CORP.
PIPER CAPITAL MANAGEMENT
PREMIER INVESTMENT ADVISORS
PRIMECAP MANAGEMENT
 COMPANY
PROVIDENT INVESTMENT COUNSEL
PUTNAM INVESTMENTS
RAINIER INVESTMENT
 MANAGEMENT
REICH & TANG CAPITAL
 MANAGEMENT
RICE, HALL, JAMES & ASSOCIATES
RICHARD FONTAINE ASSOCIATES,
 INC.
RIMCO

ROBERTSON, STEPHENS
 INVESTMENT MANAGEMENT,
 INC.
ROGER ENGEMANN & ASSOCIATES,
 INC.
RYBACK MANAGEMENT CORP.
SALOMAN BROTHERS ASSET
 MANAGEMENT, INC.
SANTA BARBARA CAPITAL
 MANAGEMENT
SCUDDER, STEVENS & CLARK, INC.
SECURITY MANAGEMENT
 COMPANY, INC.
SHAWMUT NATIONAL CORP.
SOCIETY ASSET MANAGEMENT,
 INC.
SPARE, KAPLAN, BISCHEL &
 ASSOCIATES
SPEARS, BENZAK, SALOMON &
 FARRELL
STATE STREET RESEARCH
STERLING CAPITAL MANAGEMENT
T. ROWE PRICE ASSOCIATES, INC.
TCW GROUP, INC.
TEMPLETON INTERNATIONAL
THOMPSON, SIEGEL & WALMSLEY,
 INC.
TOCQUEVILLE ASSET
 MANAGEMENT, LP
TRANSAMERICA FUND
 MANAGEMENT COMPANY
VALUE LINE ASSET MANAGEMENT
THE VANGUARD GROUP
VOYAGEUR ASSET MANAGEMENT
WADELL & REED, INC.
WAGNER ASSET MANAGEMENT, LP
WARBURG, PINCUS COUNSELLORS,
 INC.
WAYNE HUMMER INVESTMENT
 MANAGEMENT COMPANY
WEISS, PECK & GREER
WELLINGTON MANAGEMENT
 COMPANY
WELLS FARGO ASSET
 MANAGEMENT DIVISION
WOODBRIDGE CAPITAL
 MANAGEMENT
WORLD ASSET MANAGEMENT

INSURANCE COMPANIES:

ACACIA MUTUAL LIFE INSURANCE
    COMPANY
AELTUS INVESTMENT
    MANAGEMENT, INC.
AETNA LIFE GUARANTEED
    PRODUCTS GROUP
AID ASSOCIATION FOR LUTHERANS
ALABAMA REASSURANCE
    COMPANY, INC.
ALEXANDER HAMILTON LIFE INS.
    CO. OF AMERICA
ALLIANZ LIFE INS. CO. OF NORTH
    AMERICA
ALLSTATE INSURANCE COMPANY
AMERICAN BANKERS LIFE
    ASSURANCE CO. OF FLORIDA
AMERICAN FAMILY LIFE
    INSURANCE CO.
AMERICAN FIDELITY ASSURANCE
    COMPANY
AMERICAN GENERAL LIFE AND
    ACCIDENT INS. CO.
AMERICAN HERITAGE LIFE INS. CO.
AMERICAN LIFE AND ACCIDENT
    INS. CO. OF KENTUCKY
AMERICAN LIFE AND CASUALTY
    INS. CO.
AMERICAN LIFE INSURANCE
    COMPANY
AMERICAN MUTUAL LIFE
    INSURANCE COMPANY
AMERICAN NATIONAL INSURANCE
    COMPANY
AMERICAN UNITED LIFE
    INSURANCE COMPANY
AMERITAS INVESTMENT ADVISORS,
    INC.
AMEX LIFE ASSURANCE COMPANY
ANCHOR NATIONAL LIFE
    INSURANCE COMPANY
AON ADVISORS, INC.
BANKERS LIFE & CASUALTY
    COMPANY
BANKERS UNITED LIFE ASSURANCE
    COMPANY
BENEFICIAL LIFE INSURANCE
    COMPANY

BLUE CROSS & BLUE SHIELD OF
    CONNECTICUT, INC.
BLUE CROSS & BLUE SHIELD OF
    KANSAS, INC.
BLUE CROSS & BLUE SHIELD OF
    NEBRASKA
BLUE CROSS & BLUE SHIELD OF
    TEXAS, INC.
BSC LIFE INSURANCE COMPANY
BUSINESS MEN'S ASSURANCE
    COMPANY OF AMERICA
CANADA LIFE INSURANCE
    COMPANY OF AMERICA
CARILLON ADVISERS, INC.
CENTRAL NATIONAL LIFE
    INSURANCE COMPANY OF
    OMAHA
CENTRAL STATES HEALTH & LIFE
    COMPANY OF OMAHA
CENTURION LIFE INSURANCE
    COMPANY
CENTURY INVESTMENT
    MANAGEMENT CO.
CENTURY LIFE OF AMERICA
THE CHUBB CORPORATION
CINCINNATI LIFE INSURANCE
    COMPANY
CNA INSURANCE COMPANIES
COLONIAL LIFE & ACCIDENT
    INSURANCE COMPANY
COLUMBUS LIFE INSURANCE
    COMPANY
COMBINED LIFE INSURANCE
    COMPANY OF NEW YORK
CONNECTICUT GENERAL LIFE INS.
    CO.
CONNECTICUT MUTUAL LIFE
    INSURANCE COMPANY
    FINANCIAL SERVICES
CONTINENTAL ASSET
    MANAGEMENT CORP.
CONTINENTAL ASSURANCE
    COMPANY
COUNTRY LIFE INSURANCE
    COMPANY
EQUITABLE LIFE ASSURANCE
    SOCIETY OF THE U.S.

FARM BUREAU LIFE INSURANCE COMPANY

FARMERS NEW WORLD LIFE INSURANCE COMPANY

FIRST AUSA LIFE INSURANCE COMPANY

FIRST COLONY LIFE INSURANCE COMPANY

FIRST UNUM LIFE INSURANCE COMPANY

FORTIS BENEFITS INSURANCE COMPANY

FRANKLIN LIFE INSURANCE COMPANY

GENERAL AMERICAN LIFE INSURANCE CO.

GENERAL FIDELITY LIFE INSURANCE COMPANY

GOLDEN RULE INSURANCE COMPANY

GREAT AMERICAN INSURANCE COMPANIES

GREAT WEST LIFE ASSURANCE COMPANIES

GUARDIAN LIFE INSURANCE COMPANY OF AMERICA

GULF LIFE INSURANCE COMPANY

HARTFORD LIFE INSURANCE COMPANY

HEALTHCARE SERVICE GROUP

HEALTHY ALLIANCE LIFE INSURANCE COMPANY

HOME BENEFICIAL LIFE INSURANCE COMPANY

IASD HEALTH SERVICES CORP.

ILLINOIS MUTUAL LIFE INSURANCE COMPANY

INDEPENDENT LIFE & ACCIDENT INSURANCE CO.

THE INVESTMENT CENTRE, INC.

ITT HARTFORD INSURANCE GROUP

JACKSON NATIONAL LIFE INSURANCE COMPANY

JC PENNEY LIFE INSURANCE COMPANY

JEFFERSON-PILOT LIFE INSURANCE COMPANY

JOHN ALDEN LIFE INSURANCE COMPANY

JOHN HANCOCK MUTUAL LIFE INSURANCE COMPANY

KANSAS CITY LIFE INSURANCE COMPANY

KEMPER INVESTORS LIFE INSURANCE COMPANY

LIBERTY LIFE INSURANCE COMPANY

LIFE INSURANCE COMPANY OF NORTH AMERICA

LIFE INSURANCE COMPANY OF VIRGINIA

LIFE INVESTORS INSURANCE COMPANY OF AMERICA

LINCOLN NATIONAL LIFE INSURANCE COMPANY

LONE STAR LIFE INSURANCE COMPANY

MASSACHUSETTS MUTUAL LIFE INSURANCE COMPANY

MBL LIFE ASSURANCE COMPANY

MERRILL LYNCH LIFE INSURANCE COMPANY

METLIFE

MID-CONTINENT LIFE INSURANCE COMPANY

MIDLAND NATIONAL LIFE INSURANCE COMPANY

MINNESOTA MUTUAL LIFE INSURANCE COMPANY

MUTUAL LIFE INSURANCE COMPANY OF NEW YORK

MUTUAL OF OMAHA & UNITED OF OMAHA INSURANCE COMPANIES

MUTUAL SERVICE LIFE INSURANCE COMPANY

NATIONAL LIFE INSURANCE COMPANY

NATIONAL WESTERN LIFE INSURANCE COMPANY

NATIONWIDE INSURANCE GROUP

NEW ENGLAND MUTUAL LIFE INSURANCE COMPANY

NEW YORK LIFE INSURANCE CO.

NORTHWESTERN MUTUAL LIFE
INSURANCE COMPANY
NORTHWESTERN NATIONAL LIFE
INSURANCE COMPANY
OHIO CASUALTY GROUP
OHIO NATIONAL LIFE INSURANCE
COMPANY
OHIO STATE LIFE INSURANCE
COMPANY
PACIFIC MUTUAL LIFE INSURANCE
COMPANY
PAN-AMERICAN LIFE INSURANCE
COMPANY
PAUL REVERE LIFE INSURANCE
COMPANY
PENN MUTUAL LIFE INSURANCE
COMPANY
PFL LIFE INSURANCE COMPANY
PHOENIX HOME LIFE MUTUAL LIFE
INSURANCE CO.
PHYSICIANS MUTUAL INSURANCE
COMPANY
PREFERRED RISK LIFE INSURANCE
COMPANY
PRESIDENTIAL LIFE INSURANCE
COMPANY
THE PRINCIPAL FINANCIAL GROUP
PROTECTIVE LIFE INSURANCE
COMPANY
PROVIDENT LIFE & ACCIDENT
INSURANCE COMPANY
PROVIDENT MUTUAL LIFE INS. CO.
OF PHILADELPHIA
PROVIDIAN CORPORATION
THE PRUDENTIAL ASSET
MANAGEMENT GROUP
PRUDENTIAL INSURANCE
COMPANY OF AMERICA
RELIABLE LIFE INSURANCE
COMPANY
RELIANCE STANDARD LIFE
INSURANCE COMPANY
SAFECO CORPORATION
THE ST. PAUL COMPANIES, INC.
SENTRY INVESTMENT
MANAGEMENT, INC.
SOUTHERN FARM BUREAU LIFE
INSURANCE COMPANY

STANDARD INSURANCE COMPANY
STATE FARM LIFE INSURANCE
COMPANY
STATE MUTUAL OF AMERICA
TIAA-CREF
TRANSAMERICA OCCIDENTAL LIFE
INSURANCE COMPANY
THE TRAVELERS INSURANCE CO.
TRIGON BLUE CROSS BLUE SHIELD
TRUSTMARK INSURANCE
COMPANY
UNION FIDELITY LIFE INSURANCE
COMPANY
UNION LABOR LIFE INS. COMPANY
UNITED INSURANCE COMPANY OF
AMERICA
UNITED OF OMAHA LIFE
INSURANCE COMPANY
UNUM LIFE INSURANCE COMPANY
OF AMERICA
USAA LIFE INSURANCE COMPANY
USLIFE ADVISERS, INC.
VARIABLE ANNUITY LIFE
INSURANCE COMPANY
WESTERN-SOUTHERN LIFE
ASSURANCE COMPANY

BANK TRUSTS:

ALMALGA TR COMPANY
AMALGAMATED BK OF NEW YORK
AMERICAN NATIONAL BK & TR OF
MUNCIE
AMSOUTH BANK
ANB INVESTMENT MANAGEMENT &
TR COMPANY
BANCOKLAHOMA TR COMPANY
BANK IV
BANK IV OKLAHOMA
THE BANK OF NEW YORK
BANK OF THE WEST TR &
FINANCIAL SERVICES
BANK ONE, WV - CHARLESTON
BANK SOUTH, NA
BESSEMER TR COMPANY, NA
BOATMEN'S TR COMPANY
BROWN BROTHERS HARRIMANN &
CO.
BRYN MAWR TR COMPANY

CAPITAL GUARDIAN TR COMPANY
CASCO NORTHERN BK, NA
THE CENTRAL JERSEY BANK & TR
    COMPANY
CHASE MANHATTAN BK, NA
CHICAGO CITY BK & TR COMPANY
CHITTENDEN BANK
CITIBANK, NA
CITIZEN'S COMMERCIAL &
    SAVINGS BK
COLUMBUS BK & TR COMPANY
COMERICA BK
COMMERCE BK
COMMERCIAL NATIONAL BK
CORE STATES TR & INVESTMENT
    GROUP
CRESTAR BK, NA
DAIWA BK & TR COMPANY
DEPOSIT GUARANTY NATIONAL BK
FIDUCIARY TR COMPANY
    INTERNATIONAL
FIRST BANK—ASSET MANAGEMENT
    TRUST DIVISION
FIRST BK OF SOUTH DAKOTA
FIRST CITIZENS BK & TR COMPANY
FIRST CITIZENS NATIONAL BANK
FIRST COMMERCE INVESTORS
FIRST COMMERCIAL TR COMPANY,
    NA
FIRST FIDELITY BANCORPORATION
FIRST INTERSTATE BK OF ARIZONA,
    NA
FIRST INTERSTATE BANK OF
    CASPER
FIRST INTERSTATE BK OF
    CALIFORNIA
FIRST INTERSTATE BK OF
    WASHINGTON, NA
FIRST MIDWEST TR COMPANY
FIRST NATIONAL BK IN GRAND
    FORKS
FIRST NATIONAL OF BLUEFIELD
FIRST NATIONAL BK OF GLEN
    FALLS
FIRST NATIONAL BK OF LUBBOCK
FIRST NATIONAL BK OF OMAHA
FIRST NATIONAL BK OF
    SPRINGFIELD

FIRST SOURCE BK
FIRST TENNESSEE BK - KNOXVILLE
FIRST TENNESSEE BK - MEMPHIS
FIRST UNION NATIONAL BK
FIRST VICTORIA NATIONAL BANK
FIRST WESTERN TR SERVICES
    COMPANY
FIRSTAR BANK DES MOINES, NA
FIRSTAR BANK SHEBOYGAN, NA
FIRSTIER BK (LINCOLN)
FLEET INVESTMENT ADVISORS,
    INC.
FORT WAYNE NATIONAL BK
FUJI BK & TR COMPANY
GROOS BANK, NA
HERITAGE PULLMAN BK & TR
    COMPANY
HIBERNIA NATIONAL BK
HUNTINGTON TR COMPANY
    (CLEVELAND)
HUNTINGTON TR COMPANY
    (COLUMBUS)
INTRUST BK, NA
JEFFERSON NATIONAL BK
KEY TR COMPANY (ALBANY, NY)
LAFAYETTE BK & TR COMPANY
LASALLE NATIONAL TRUST, NA
LUFKIN NATIONAL BK
MAHONING NATIONAL BK OF
    YOUNGSTOWN
MECHANICS BANK OF RICHMOND
MELLON TRUST
MIDATLANTIC BK, NA
NATIONAL BK OF ALASKA
NATIONAL WESTMINSTER BK
NAZARETH NATIONAL BK & TR
    COMPANY
NBD BANK, NA
NEW JERSEY NATIONAL BK
NORTH CENTRAL TRUST COMPANY
NORTHERN TR COMPANY
NORWEST BK INDIANA, NA
NORWEST BK MINNESOTA, NA
NORWEST CAPITAL MANAGEMENT
    & TRUST COMPANY
    MONTANA
NORWEST INVESTMENTS & TR
    COMPANY OF WISCONSIN

OLD STONE TR COMPANY
PNC BK CORPORATION
PREMIER BK (BATON ROUGE)
PREMIER BK (SHREVEPORT)
REPUBLIC NATIONAL BK OF NEW
    YORK
RHODE ISLAND HOSPITAL TR
    NATIONAL BK
SANTA MONICA BK
SANWA TRUST
STAR BK, EASTERN INDIANA, NA
SUMITOMO BK OF CALIFORNIA
SUN BANK CAPITAL MANAGEMENT,
    NA
THIRD NATIONAL BK IN NASHVILLE
TRUSTCO BK
TRUST COMPANY OF OKLAHOMA
U. S. TR COMPANY
U.S. TR COMPANY OF NEW YORK
UMB COMMERCIAL NATIONAL BK
UNION CAPITAL ADVISORS
UNION TR COMPANY
UNITED NATIONAL BK
    (CHARLESTON, WV)
UNITED STATES COMPANY OF
    BOSTON
UNITED STATES TR COMPANY OF
    TEXAS, NA
VICTORIA BK & TRUST COMPANY
WACHOVIA INVESTMENT
    MANAGEMENT
WELLS FARGO DEFINED
    CONTRIBUTION TRUST
    COMPANY
WILMINGTON TR COMPANY
WORTHEN BK & TR COMPANY

FOUNDATIONS:

AARON STRAUS & LILLIE STRAUS
    FOUNDATION, INC.
AMELIA PEABODY CHARITABLE
    FUND
AMELIA PEABODY FOUNDATION
AMOCO FOUNDATION, INC.
AMON G. CARTER FOUNDATION
ARNOLD & MABEL BECKMAN
    FOUNDATION
BARRA FOUNDATION, INC.

BOOTH FERRIS FOUNDATION
BRADLEY-TURNER FOUNDATION
BUHL FOUNDATION
BULLITT FOUNDATION
CAPITAL FUND FOUNDATION
CASTELLINI FOUNDATION
CHARLES ENGELHARD
    FOUNDATION
CHARLES HAYDEN FOUNDATION
CHARLES STEWART MOTT
    FOUNDATION
CHEROKEE FOUNDATION, INC
CLARK FOUNDATION
COLUMBIA FOUNDATION
COMMUNITY FOUNDATION OF
    SOUTHEASTERN MICHIGAN
COMMUNITY FOUNDATION OF
    ELMIRA-CORNING AREA
COMMUNITY FOUNDATION OF
    GREATER NEW HAVEN
COTTRELL FOUNDATION
CRAIL-JOHNSON FOUNDATION
DANIEL FOUNDATION OF ALABAMA
DANIEL & JOANNA S. ROSE FUND,
    INC.
DAVID & SADIE KLAU FOUNDATION
DIETRICH FOUNDATION, INC.
DR. SCHOLL FOUNDATION
E.M. PEARSON FOUNDATION
EDEN HALL FOUNDATION
EDWIN GOULD FOUNDATION FOR
    CHILDREN
EFFIE & WOFFORD CAIN
    FOUNDATION
EISENBERG FUND FOR CHARITIES
ELINOR PATTERSON BAKER
    FOUNDATION
F.J. O'NEILL CHARITABLE
    CORPORATION
FORD FOUNDATION
FOUNDATION FOR THE CHARITIES
FRANK E. PAYNE & SEBA B. PAYNE
    FOUNDATION
FREEDOM FORUM INTERNATIONAL
    INC
FULLER E. CALLAWAY FOUNDATION
GAR FOUNDATION

GEORGE W. JENKINS FOUNDATION, INC.
GEORGE W. BARBER, JR. FOUNDATION
GLAXO WELLCOME FOUNDATION
H.N. & FRANCES C. BERGER FOUNDATION (DELAWARE)
HAL & CHARLIE PETERSON FOUNDATION
HALL FOUNDATION, INC.
HARRY C. MOORES FOUNDATION
HARRY C. TREXLER TRUST
HELEN K. & ARTHUR E. JOHNSON FOUNDATION
HELENE FULD HEALTH TRUST
HENRY J. KAISER FAMILY FOUNDATION
HOUSTON ENDOWMENT, INC.
HOWARD HUGHES MEDICAL INSTITUTE
I.A. O'SHAUGHESSY FOUNDATION, INC.
IRVING A. HANSEN MEMORIAL FOUNDATION
IRVING S. GILMORE FOUNDATION
J. WEINSTEIN FOUNDATION, INC.
J. WILLARD MARRIOTT FOUNDATION
J.S. BIRDWELL FOUNDATION
JESSIE SMITH NOYES FOUNDATION, INC.
JOHN D. & CATHERINE T. MACARTHUR FOUNDATION
JOHN P. MCGOVERN FOUNDATION
JOHN & MARY R. MARKLE FOUNDATION
JOSIAH MACY, JR. FOUNDATION
KATE B. REYNOLDS CHARITABLE TRUST
LAKESIDE FOUNDATION
LEVI STRAUSS FOUNDATION
LIED FOUNDATION TRUST
LILA WALLACE - READERS DIGEST FUND, INC.
LIZ CLAIBORNE & ART ORTENBERG FOUNDATION
LOUIS R. LAURIE FOUNDATION
LYNDHURST FOUNDATION

M.E. RINKER, SR. FOUNDATION, INC.
MARIN COMMUNITY FOUNDATION
MARK IV INDUSTRIES FOUNDATION, INC.
MARTY & DOROTHY SILVERMAN FOUNDATION
MAX KADE FOUNDATION, INC.
MCLEOD BLUE SKYE CHARITABLE FOUNDATION
MEYER MEMORIAL TRUST
MILLKEN FAMILY FOUNDATION
MILWAUKEE FOUNDATION
MORIAH FUND
MORLEY BROTHERS FOUNDATION
NATHAN FOUNDATION, INC.
NELDA C. & H.J. LUTCHER STARK FOUNDATION
NEW YORK COMMUNITY TRUST
NYNEX FOUNDATION
ORVILLE D. & RUTH A. MERILLAT FOUNDATION
OTTO BREMER FOUNDATION
PEABODY FOUNDATION, INC.
PHILIP H. CORBOY FOUNDATION
PHILIP L. GRAHAM FUND
PRESBYTERIAN HEALTH FOUNDATION
R. J. MCELROY TRUST
R.K. MELLON FAMILY FOUNDATION
RESEARCH CORPORATION
RICHARD KING MELLON FOUNDATION
ROBERT M. BEREN FOUNDATION, INC.
ROBERT W. WOODRUFF FOUNDATION, INC.
ROBERT G. CABELL III & MAUDE MORGAN CABELL
ROCKEFELLER BROTHERS FUND
S.H. COWELL FOUNDATION
SAGE FOUNDATION
SAINT PAUL FOUNDATION, INC.
SAN DIEGO COMMUNITY FOUNDATION
SARAH SCAIFE FOUNDATION, INC.
SETH SPRAGUE EDUCATIONAL & CHARITABLE FOUNDATION
SIMMS FOUNDATION

SLEMP FOUNDATION
SMITH RICHARDSON FOUNDATION, INC.
SMITHKLINE BEECHAM FOUNDATION
SOROS HUMANITARIAN FOUNDATION
TED MANN FOUNDATION
TELESIS FOUNDATION
TOWN CREEK FOUNDATION, INC.
UNITED STATES ADVOCATES FOR YOUTH FOUNDATION
W. PARSONS TODD FOUNDATION, INC.
W.M. KECK FOUNDATION
WALTER SCOTT JR. FOUNDATION
WALTER & ELISE HAAS FUND
WEINGART FOUNDATION
WILBUR MAY FOUNDATION
WILLIAM & FLORA HEWETT FOUNDATION
WOOD-RILL FOUNDATION

ENDOWMENTS:

ABILENE CHRISTIAN UNIVERSITY
ALBRIGHT COLLEGE
ALLEGHENY COLLEGE
AMHERST COLLEGE
ANGELO STATE UNIVERSITY
AUBURN UNIVERSITY
AUGUSTANA COLLEGE
BALTIMORE SYMPHONY ORCHESTRA
BARNARD COLLEGE
BEREA COLLEGE
THE BLAKE SCHOOL
BOSTON UNIVERSITY
BRADLEY UNIVERSITY
BROWN UNIVERSITY
BUTLER UNIVERSITY
CAMPBELL UNIVERSITY
CARNEGIE INSTITUTION OF WASHINGTON
CARROLL COLLEGE
CHAPMAN UNIVERSITY
CINCINNATI SYMPHONY ORCHESTRA
CLAREMONT MCKENNA COLLEGE

CLEMSON UNIVERSITY FOUNDATION
CLEVELAND INSTITUTE OF ART
COLLEGE OF WILLIAM & MARY
COLUMBIA UNIVERSITY
CRANBROOK EDUCATIONAL COMMUNITY
DAVIS & ELKINS COLLEGE
DEPAUW UNIVERSITY
DETROIT INSTITUTE OF ARTS
DOANE COLLEGE
ELIZABETHTOWN COLLEGE
EMORY UNIVERSITY
FAIRFIELD UNIVERSITY
FLORIDA STATE UNIVERSITY
FLORIDA COLLEGE
FURMAN UNIVERSITY
GMI ENGINEERING & MANAGEMENT INSTITUTE
GRINNELL COLLEGE
GROTON SCHOOL
GUILFORD COLLEGE
HILL SCHOOL
HOPE COLLEGE
HOTCHKISS SCHOOL
HOWARD UNIVERSITY
HUNTINGTON COLLEGE
JOHN HOPKINS UNIVERSITY
KALAMAZOO COLLEGE
KENT SCHOOL CORPORATION
KNOX COLLEGE
LAFAYETTE COLLEGE
LENOIR RHYNE COLLEGE
LOOMIS CHAFFEE SCHOOL
LOYOLA MARYMOUNT UNIVERSITY
MACALESTER COLLEGE
MADEIRA SCHOOL
MAY INSTITUTE & ST. LOUIS COUNTRY DAY SCHOOL
MCDONOGH SCHOOL
METROPOLITAN MUSEUM OF ART
MIAMI-DADE COMMUNITY COLLEGE
MIDDLEBURY COLLEGE
MISSISSIPPI COLLEGE
MISSISSIPPI STATE UNIVERSITY
MOUNT UNION COLLEGE

Appendix C
LIST OF INSTITUTIONAL OWNER FOR SECOND SURVEY

PUBLIC PENSION PLANS:

THE R.S. OF ALABAMA

ALAMEDA-CONTRA COSTA
  TRANSIT DISTRICT

ALPENA EMPLOYEE'S RETIREMENT
  SYSTEM

AMARILLO FIREMEN'S RELIEF &
  RETIREMENT FUND

ARKANSAS STATE POLICE R.S.

THE ARMY & AIR FORCE
  EXCHANGE SERVICE

BEAVER COUNTY EMPLOYEES'
  RETIREMENT FUND

BIRMINGHAM R.S.

BRAINTREE CONTRIBUTORY R.S.

BRIDGEVIEW POLICE PENSION
  FUND

BURLINGTON EMPLOYEES' R.S.

CITY OF NEW ORLEANS
  EMPLOYEES' R.S.

CITY OF CHICAGO DEFERRED
  COMPENSATION PLAN

CITY OF DEERFIELD BEACH R.S.

COLORADO PUBLIC EMPLOYEES'
  RETIREMENT ASSOCIATION

CORAL GABLES R.S.

COVINGTON POLICE & FIREMEN
  PENSION FUND

DENVER PUBLIC SCHOOL
  EMPLOYEES' PENSION &
  BENEFIT ASSOCIATION

DES MOINES TEACHERS' R.S.

DOTHAN EMPLOYEES' PENSION &
  BENEFIT FUND

FARGO FIREMEN'S RELIEF
  ASSOCIATION

FERNDALE R.S.

FIREMEN'S RELIEF & RETIREMENT
  PLAN CITY OF WICHITA
  FALLS

FRESNO CITY EMPLOYEES' R.S.

FULTON COUNTY SCHOOL PENSION
  FUND

GEORGIA FIREMEN'S PENSION
  FUND

HAMILTON COUNTY RETIREMENT
  SYSTEM

IDAHO PUBLIC EMPLOYEE R.S.

INDIANA STATE POLICE PENSION
  FUND

IOWA PEACE OFFICERS' R.S.

IOWA PUBLIC EMPLOYEES' R.S.

JACKSONVILLE CITY R.S.

KANSAS CITY EMPLOYEES &
  POLICE R.S.

KENTUCKY JUDICIAL R.S.

LAFAYETTE POLICE/FIRE PENSION
  & RELIEF FUND

LANCASTER COUNTY EMPLOYEES'
  RETIREMENT FUND

LEXINGTON-FACETTE URBAN
  COUNTY GOVERNMENT

LOS ANGELES COUNTY
  METROPOLITAN TRANSIT
  AUTHORITY

LOUISIANA TEACHERS' R.S.

MADISON HEIGHTS POLICE & FIRE
  R.S.

MARYLAND NATIONAL CAPITAL
  PARK &

MATTOON POLICE & FIREMEN'S
  PENSION FUNDS

METROPOLITAN WATER
  RECLAMATION DISTRICT
  RETIREMENT FUND

MID-SOUTH TRANSPORTATION
  MANAGEMENT, INC. (MIM)

MINNEAPOLIS EMPLOYEES'
  RETIREMENT FUND

MINNEAPOLIS FIRE DEPARTMENT
  RELIEF ASSOCIATION

MISSOURI STATE EMPLOYEES' R.S.

NASHVILLE METROPOLITAN
  PUBLIC SCHOOLS

NEBRASKA PUBLIC EMPLOYEES'
  R.S.

NEW YORK STATE DEFERRED
  COMPENSATION BOARD

NEW HAMPSHIRE R.S.

NORFOLK POLICE, FIRE AND
  CIVILIANS PENSION FUND

NORMAN CITY RETIREMENT
   SYSTEM (R.S.)
ODESSA FIREMEN'S RELIEF
   RETIREMENT FUND
OHIO STATE HIGHWAY PATROL R.S.
OHIO STATE TEACHERS' R.S.
PENNSYLVANIA STATE EMPLOYEES'
   R.S.
PLANNING COMMISSION
   EMPLOYEES' R.S.
POLICE & GENERAL EMPLOYEES'
   PENSION PLANS—CITY OF
   HALLANDALE
PRAIRIE VILLAGE POLICE
   DEPARTMENT PENSION PLAN
PROVIDENCE EMPLOYEES' R.S.
SAN BERNARDINO COUNTY
   EMPLOYEES' RETIREMENT
   ASSOCIATION
SAN LUIS OBISPO COUNTY
   RETIREMENT PLANS
SOUTHEASTERN PENNSYLVANIA
   TRANSPORTATION
   AUTHORITY
SPARTANBURG RETIREMENT
   SYSTEMS
SPOKANE EMPLOYEES' R.S.
ST. LOUIS EMPLOYEES' R.S.
THE FIREMEN'S R.S. OF ST. LOUIS
TACOMA EMPLOYEES' R.S.
TENNESSEE VALLEY AUTHORITY
   R.S.
TRANSIT MANAGEMENT OF
   SOUTHEAST LOUISIANA
   (TMSEL)
TYLER FIREMEN'S RELIEF R.S.
UNIVERSITY CITY POLICE &
   FIREMEN'S R.S.
UTAH STATE R.S.
WASHINGTON METRO AREA
   TRANSIT AUTHORITY
   RETIREMENT PLANS
WATERBURY R.S.
WILMINGTON PENSION SYSTEM
WYOMING CITY EMPLOYEES' R.S.
WYOMING R.S.

PRIVATE PENSION PLANS:

ABBOTT LABORATORIES
AFFILIATED FOODS, INC.
AMERICAN ASSOCIATION OF
   ADVERTISING AGENCIES
AMERICAN MANUFACTURING CORP.
AMGEN
AMOCO CORPORATION
ARMSTRONG WORLD INDUSTRIES
ARVIN INDUSTRIES, INC.
ASSOCIATED BENEFITS
   CORPORATION
AVON PRODUCTS, INC.
BAKER HUGHES, INC.
BANDAG INCORPORATED
THE BARDEN CORPORATION
BARNHARDT MANUFACTURING CO.
BEHLEN MANUFACTURING CO.
BELDING HEMINGWAY CO., INC.
BERKLEY, INC..
BEVERLY ENTERPRISES
BOSTON EDISON COMPANY
BOWATER, INC.
BOZELL JACOBS
BROWN GROUP, INC
BUTLER MANUFACTURING CO.
CABELAS, INC.
CH2M HILL INC.
CHIEF INDUSTRIES, INC.
THE COASTAL CORPORATION
COMMERCIAL FEDERAL BANK
DALE ELECTRONICS
DATA DOCUMENTS, INC.
DEERE & COMPANY
DEXTER CO., INC..
DI GIORGIO CORPORATION
DRESSER INDUSTRIES, INC.
DUKE POWER COMPANY
DYNATECH CORPORATION
EASTERS, INC.
ELCO INDUSTRIES, INC.
ELECTRICAL ENGINEERING &
   EQUIPMENT CO.
EMCO INDUSTRIES, INC.
EMERSON ELECTRIC CO.
ENSERCH CORP.
FARMLAND INDUSTRIES, INC.
FLEMING COMPANIES, INC.

FLEXSTEEL INDUSTRIES, INC..
FMC CORP.
FOODS, INC.
GENERAL GROWTH COMPANIES
THE GILETTE COMPANY
GREYHOUND AMALGAMATED
    TRUSTS
HANSEN, LIND, MEYER INC..
HARNISCHFEGER INDUSTRIES, INC.
HASBRO, INC.
HDR, INC.
HERCULES, INC.
HOECHST CELANESE CORPORATION
HOLMES MURPHY & ASSOCIATES
    INC..
HON INDUSTRIES, INC..
IBP, INC.
ICI SEEDS
IMT INSURANCE CO.
THE INTERNATIONAL MONETARY
    FUND
INTERSTATE POWER COMPANY
IOWA ASSOCIATION OF ELECTRIC
    COOPERATIVES
IOWA REALTY CO., INC..
ISCO, INC.
JOURNAL STAR PRINTING CO.
K-PRODUCTS, INC..
KAMAN CORP.
KIRKE-VAN ORSDEL, INC..
KN ENERGY, INC.
LEGGETT & PLATT, INC.
LEO A. DALY CO.
LINDSAY MANUFACTURING CO.
LOCKWOOD CORPORATION
LOZIER CORPORATION
LYMAN-RICHEY SAND & GRAVEL
MARION MERRILL DOW, INC.
MARRIOTT INTERNATIONAL
    CORPORATION
MAY DEPARTMENT STORES
    COMPANY
MAYTAG CORPORATION
MEREDITH CORPORATION
METROMAIL CORPORATION
METZ BAKING CO.
MFA OIL COMPANY
MICHELIN TIRE CORP.

MID-AMERICA TRUST COMPANY
MIDLAND LUTHERAN COLLEGE
MIDWEST POWER SYSTEMS, INC..
MILLER ELECTRIC
    MANUFACTURING COMPANY
MONSANTO COMPANY
MURPHY OIL CORPORATION
NATIONAL BY-PRODUCTS, INC.
NEBCO, INC.
NEBRASKA PUBLIC POWER
    DISTRICT
NEWTON MANUFACTURING CO.
NIBCO INC.
NOBLE AFFILIATES, INC.
NYEMASTER, GOODE,
    MCLAUGHLIN, EMERY &
    O'BRIEN, P.C
PACESETTER CORP.
PAMIDA, INC.
PAYLESS CASHWAYS, INC.
PELLA CORPORATION
THE PERRIER GROUP
PETERSEN MANUFACTURING CO.,
    INC.
PHILLIPS ELECTRONICS NORTH
    AMERICA CORPORATION
PHILLIPS PETROLEUM COMPANY
PIONEER HI-BRED INTERNATIONAL,
    INC.
ROBERTS & DYBDAHL, INC.
RUAN TRANSPORT CORP.
SCHILDBERG CONSTRUCTION
SEALY CORPORATION
SECURITY NATIONAL CORP.
SHEAFFER INC.
SHELL OIL COMPANY
SHERWIN-WILLIAMS COMPANY
SIOUX TOOLS, INC.
STANLEY CONSULTANTS, INC.
THE STATESMAN GROUP, INC.
STORE KRAFT MANUFACTURING
    CO.
TENNECO, INC.
TERRA INDUSTRIES, INC.
TEXTRON, INC.
TOWNSEND ENGINEERING CO.
TRANSCO ENERGY COMPANY
UNITED AGRISEEDS, INC..

UNITED A.G. COOPERATIVE, INC.
UNITED TECHNOLOGIES
UST INC.
VARIED INDUSTRIES, INC..
VERMEER MANUFACTURING CO.
VERNON COMPANY
VOLVO CARS OF NORTH AMERICA,
    INC.
WARREN TRANSPORT, INC.
WATERLOO WATERWORKS
THE WEITZ CORPORATION
WELLS DAIRY, INC.
WERNER ENTERPRISES, INC.
WILLIAM C. BROWN CO.,
    PUBLISHERS
WILSON TRAILER CO., INC.
WINNEBAGO INDUSTRIES, INC.
YOUNKERS, INC.

PRIVATE PLANS / UNION PLANS

AMERICAN FEDERATION OF STATE,
    COUNTY & MUNICIPAL
    EMPLOYEES
AMERICAN FEDERATION OF LABOR
    & CONGRESS OF INDUSTRIAL
    ORGANIZATION
ASBESTOS WORKERS, LOCAL #32
ASBESTOS WORKERS, LOCAL #39
BAKERY & CONFECTIONARY UNION
BAKERY, CONFECTIONERY &
    TOBACCO WORKERS, LOCAL
    #433
CARPENTERS PENSION FUND OF
    ILLINOIS
CARPENTERS, LOCAL #948
CARPENTERS, DISTRICT COUNCIL,
    NEW YORK CITY
CARPENTERS, STATE COUNCIL,
    WISCONSIN
ELECTRICAL WORKERS, IBEW,
    INTERNATIONAL
    HEADQUARTERS
ELECTRICAL WORKERS, IBEW,
    LOCAL #86
ELECTRICAL WORKERS, IBEW,
    LOCAL #332
ELECTRICAL WORKERS, IBEW,
    LOCAL #347

ENGINEERS, OPERATING,
    INTERNATIONAL
FOOD & COMMERCIAL WORKERS,
    LOCAL #888
FOOD & COMMERCIAL WORKERS,
    SOUTHERN CALIFORNIA
    LOCALS
HOTEL & RESTAURANT
    EMPLOYEES, LOCAL #165
    INDUSTRY INTERNATIONAL
    PENSION FUND
INTERNATIONAL ASSOCIATION OF
    MACHINISTS & AEROSPACE
    WORKERS
IRON WORKERS, LOCAL #67
LABORERS, INTERNATIONAL
    HEADQUARTERS
LABORERS, LOCAL #731
MARITIME ASSOCIATION ILA FUNDS
MIDWEST OPERATING ENGINEERS
    PENSION TRUST FUND
NATIONAL INDUSTRIAL GROUP
    PENSION PLAN
PLUMBERS, LOCAL #25
PLUMBERS, LOCAL #33
PLUMBERS, LOCAL #130
PRODUCERS-WRITERS GUILD OF
    AMERICA
SEAFARERS PENSION PLAN
TEAMSTERS, BAKERY DRIVERS
    LOCAL #550
TEAMSTERS, CENTRAL STATES,
    SOUTHEAST & SOUTHWEST
    AREAS PENSION FUND
TEAMSTERS, LOCAL #639,
    EMPLOYERS PENSION TRUST
UNITED FOOD & COMMERCIAL
    WORKERS INTERNATIONAL
    UNION
UNITED FOOD & COMMERCIAL
    WORKERS - PENSION FUND,
    ATLANTA
WINERY & ALLIED WORKERS,
    LOCAL #45

MUTUAL FUNDS / MONEY MANAGERS:

ALEX BROWN INVESTMENT
  MANAGEMENT, LP
ANALYTIC INVESTMENT
  MANAGEMENT, INC.
B OF A CAPITAL MANAGEMENT,
  INC.
BACK BAY ADVISORS, LP
BAYBANKS INVESTMENT
  MANAGEMENT, INC.
BOSTON SECURITY COUNSELLORS
BRANDES INVESTMENT PARTNERS,
  INC.
BZW INVESTMENT MANAGEMENT
  INC.
CALAMOS ASSET MANAGEMENT,
  INC.
CAPITOLINE INVESTMENT
  SERVICES, INC.
CATERPILLAR INVESTMENT
  MANAGEMENT, LTD.
THE COMMON FUND
COOKE & BIELER, INC..
CRAMBILT & CARNEY
DG ASSET MANAGEMENT GROUP
FEDERATED INVESTORS
FIRST INTERSTATE BANK OF
  CALIFORNIA
FIRST ASSET MANAGEMENT
FRANKLIN PORTFOLIO ASSOCIATES
GARDNER LEWIS ASSET
  MANAGEMENT
GLOBAL ADVISORS
HARBOR CAPITAL MANAGEMENT
  COMPANY, INC.
HARRIS INVESTMENT
  MANAGEMENT
HOTCHKIS & WILEY
INVESCO CAPITAL MANAGEMENT,
  INC..
J.P. MORGAN INVESTMENT
  MANAGEMENT, INC.
JUNDT ASSOCIATES, INC..
KEELEY ASSET MANAGEMENT
KIDDER PEABODY ASSET
  MANAGEMENT
L. ROY PAPP & ASSOCIATES

LASALLE STREET CAPITAL
  MANAGEMENT, LTD.
LLAMA ASSET MANAGEMENT
  COMPANY
LYNCH & MAYER
MATHERS & COMPANY, INC..
MELLON EQUITY ASSOCIATES
MERCATOR ASSET MANAGEMENT,
  INC.
MERUS CAPITAL MANAGEMENT
MESIROW ASSET MANAGEMENT
MISSISSIPPI VALLEY ADVISORS, INC.
MONETTA FINANCIAL SERVICES,
  INC.
MORGAN STANLEY ASSET
  MANAGEMENT
MORLEY CAPITAL MANAGEMENT
MURRAY, JOHNSTONE
  INTERNATIONAL, LTD.
NATIONAL MUTUAL FUNDS
  MANAGEMENT (NORTH
  AMERICA)
NEWBOLD'S ASSET MANAGEMENT,
  INC.
NEWELL ASSOCIATES
NEWPORT PACIFIC MANAGEMENT
NOMURA CAPITAL MANAGEMENT
PACIFIC FINANCIAL RESEARCH
  (PFR), INC.
PDI STRATEGIES
PEREGRINE CAPITAL
  MANAGEMENT, INC.
THE PORTFOLIO GROUP
SCHRODER CAPITAL MANAGEMENT
  INTERNATIONAL, INC.
SIT INVESTMENT ASSOCIATES, INC.
SMITH BARNEY CAPITAL
  MANAGEMENT
SOUND SHORE MANAGEMENT, INC.
STEIN ROE & FARNHAM
  INCORPORATED
STONEBRIDGE CAPITAL
  MANAGEMENT, INC.
SWANSON CAPITAL MANAGEMENT
TRANSAMERICA INVESTMENT
  SERVICES
WADDELL & REED, INC.

WELLINGTON MANAGEMENT
COMPANY
WELLS FARGO NIKKO INVESTMENT
ADVISORS
WESTPEAK INVESTMENT
ADVISERS, L.P.
WILLIAM BLAIR & COMPANY
WILSHIRE ASSET MANAGEMENT
WOOD ISLAND ASSOCIATES, INC..
WRIGHT INVESTORS' SERVICES
YACKTMAN ASSET MANAGEMENT
COMPANY
THE YARMOUTH GROUP

INSURANCE COMPANIES:

AELTUS INVESTMENT
MANAGEMENT, INC.
AETNA LIFE GUARANTEED
PRODUCTS GROUP
AID ASSOCIATION FOR LUTHERANS
ALLSTATE PLAZA
AMERICAN UNITED LIFE
INSURANCE COMPANY
AON ADVISORS, INC..
BENEFICIAL LIFE INSURANCE
COMPANY
CARILLON ADVISERS, INC..
CENTRAL STATES HEALTH & LIFE
COMPANY
CENTURY INVESTMENT
MANAGEMENT CO.
THE CHUBB CORPORATION
CNA INSURANCE COMPANIES
CONNECTICUT MUTUAL LIFE
INSURANCE COMPANY
CONTINENTAL ASSET
MANAGEMENT CORP.
EMPLOYERS MUTUAL CASUALTY
CO.
FARMERS MUTUAL HAIL
INSURANCE CO. OF IOWA
GENERAL AMERICAN LIFE
INSURANCE CO.
GREAT WEST LIFE ASSURANCE
COMPANY
GREAT AMERICAN INSURANCE
COMPANIES

THE INVESTMENT CENTRE, INC.
ITT HARTFORD INSURANCE GROUP
LINCOLN NATIONAL LIFE
INSURANCE COMPANY
MASSACHUSETTS MUTUAL LIFE
INSURANCE COMPANY
METLIFE
MUTUAL SERVICE LIFE INSURANCE
COMPANY
NATIONAL TRAVELERS LIFE CO.
NATIONWIDE INSURANCE GROUP
NEW YORK LIFE INSURANCE CO.
OHIO CASUALTY GROUP
OHIO NATIONAL LIFE INSURANCE
COMPANY
PAN-AMERICAN LIFE INSURANCE
COMPANY
PENN MUTUAL LIFE INSURANCE
COMPANY
PHOENIX HOME LIFE MUTUAL
INSURANCE CO.
PHYSICIANS MUTUAL INSURANCE
CO.
PM CAPITAL MANAGEMENT
PROTECTIVE LIFE INSURANCE
COMPANY
PROVIDENT MUTUAL LIFE
INSURANCE COMPANY OF
PHILADELPHIA
PROVIDENT LIFE & ACCIDENT
INSURANCE COMPANY
PROVIDIAN CORPORATION
THE PRUDENTIAL ASSET
MANAGEMENT GROUP
SAFECO CORPORATION
THE ST. PAUL COMPANIES, INC.
SECURITY MUTUAL LIFE
INSURANCE COMPANY
SENTRY INVESTMENT
MANAGEMENT, INC.
STANDARD INSURANCE COMPANY
STATE MUTUAL OF AMERICA
THE TRAVELERS INSURANCE CO.
USLIFE ADVISERS, INC.
WOODMEN ACCIDENT & LIFE
COMPANY

BANK TRUSTS:

AMERICAN NATIONAL BANK &
  TRUST COMPANY OF
  CHATTANOOGA
AMSOUTH BANK
ASSOCIATED BANK, NA
BANK OF BOSTON - CONNECTICUT
BANK OF TOKYO TRUST COMPANY
BANKER TRUST COMPANY
BANKERS TRUST COMPANY
BAYBANKS INVESTMENT
  MANAGEMENT, INC.
CAPE COD BANK & TRUST CO.
CHEMICAL BANK & TRUST
  COMPANY
CITIZENS TRUST COMPANY
CORESTATES HAMILTON BANK
DANIELSON TRUST
FIFTH THIRD BANK
FIRST ALABAMA BANK
FIRST AMERICAN TRUST COMPANY,
  NA
FIRST BANK, NA
FIRST EASTERN BANK, NA
FIRST HAWAIIAN BANK
FIRST INTERSTATE BANK OF
  DENVER, NA
FIRST INTERSTATE BANK Of
  NEVADA-TRUST
FIRST INTERSTATE BANK OF
  OREGON
FIRST NATIONAL BANK
FIRST NATIONAL BANK IN
  ALBERQUERQUE
FIRST NATIONAL BANK OF ABILENE
THE FIRST NATIONAL BANK OF
  CHICAGO
THE FIRST NATIONAL BANK OF
  DECATUR
THE FIRST NATIONAL BANK OF
  KENOSHA
THE FIRST NATIONAL BANK OF
  MARYLAND
FIRST NATIONAL BANK OF OHIO
THE FIRST NATIONAL BANK IN
  SIOUX FALLS
FIRST TENNESSEE BANK -
  CHATTANOOGA

FIRST TRUST NATIONAL
  ASSOCIATION
FIRSTAR BANK CEDAR RAPIDS, NA
FIRSTAR BANK OSHKOSH, NA
FRONT STREET CAPITAL
  MANAGEMENT
THE FROST NATIONAL BANK
THE GLENMEDE TRUST COMPANY
HARRIS TRUST & SAVINGS BANK
HAWAIIAN TRUST COMPANY, LTD.
HAWKEYE BANK & TRUST OF DES
  MOINES
THE HOWARD BANK GREAT BANC
  TRUST COMPANY
IBJ SCHRODER BANK & TRUST
  COMPANY
INTEGRA TRUST COMPANY
INTER-CITY BANK
KEY TRUST COMPANY
KEY TRUST COMPANY
LIBERTY NATIONAL BANK & TRUST
  COMPANY OF LOUISVILLE
MARSHALL & ISLEY TRUST
  COMPANY
THE MERCHANTS NATIONAL BANK
MERCANTILE BANK, NA
MERCANTILE-SAFE DEPOSIT &
  TRUST COMPANY
MICHIGAN NATIONAL BANK
THE NATIONAL BANK OF
  WATERLOO
NATIONAR
NORWEST BANK DES MOINES, NA
NORWEST BANK SOUTH DAKOTA,
  NA
NORWEST FINANCIAL, INC..
OLD NATIONAL BANK IN
  EVANSVILLE
PIEDMONT TRUST BANK
PRINCETON BANK & TRUST
  COMPANY, N.A.
PROVIDENT INVESTMENT
  ADVISORS
RCB TRUST COMPANY
THE SECOND NATIONAL BANK OF
  WARREN
SIGNET TRUST COMPANY

SOUTHTRUST ESTATE & TRUST
  COMPANY OF GEORGIA, NA
STAR BANK
STATE STREET BANK & TRUST
  COMPANY
STOCK YARDS BANK & TRUST
  COMPANY
THE SUMMIT BANK
TEXAS COMMERCE BANK, NA
TOMPKINS COUNTY TRUST
  COMPANY
UNION NATIONAL BANK OF
  WICHITA
UNITED JERSEY BANK
UNITED MISSOURI BANK OF
  KANSAS CITY, NA
UNITED STATES NATIONAL BANK
THE UNITED STATES NATIONAL
  BANK
UNITED STATES NATIONAL BANK OF
  OREGON
U..S. TRUST COMPANY OF
  CALIFORNIA, NA
WEST ONE BANK, IDAHO
ZIONS FIRST NATIONAL BANK

FOUNDATIONS:

ABEL FOUNDATION
ACKLIE CHARITABLE FOUNDATION
AHMANSON FOUNDATION
AMERITAS CHARITABLE
  FOUNDATION
ANDREW W. MELLON FOUNDATION
ARMSTRONG MCDONALD
  FOUNDATION
ARTHUR S. DEMOSS FOUNDATION
BERNARD K. & NORMA F.
  HEUERMANN FOUNDATION
BILL AND BERNIECE GREWCOCK
  FOUNDATION
BROWN FOUNDATION, INC.
BUFFETT FOUNDATION
CARL AND CAROLINE SWANSON
  FOUNDATION, INC.
CARNEGIE CORPORATION OF NEW
  YORK
CHARLES EDISON FOUNDATION
CHATLOS FOUNDATION, INC.

CLIFFORD J. MILLER CHARITABLE
  FOUNDATION
COMPTON FOUNDATION, INC.
CONAGRA FOUNDATION, INC
COOPER FOUNDATION
CORD FOUNDATION
DEL E. WEBB FOUNDATION
DONALD W. REYNOLDS
  FOUNDATION
DUKE ENDOWMENT
DURHAM FOUNDATION
EDGAR REYNOLDS FOUNDATION,
  INC.
ETHEL S. ABBOTT CHARITABLE
  FOUNDATION
EUGENE B. CASEY FOUNDATION
FRANK M. AND ALICE M. FARR
  TRUST
GARDNER FOUNDATION
GILBERT M. AND MARTHA H.
  HITCHCOCK FOUNDATION
GREATER NEW ORLEANS
  FOUNDATION
GTE FOUNDATION
HARRY & JEANETTE WEINBERG
  FOUNDATION, INC.
HAWKINS CHARITABLE TRUST
HAZEL R. KEENE TRUST
IBP FOUNDATION, INC.
IKE & ROZ FRIEDMAN FOUNDATION
JESSIE BALLOU DUPONT FUND
JOHN SIMON GUGGENHEIM
  MEMORIAL FOUNDATION
KIEWIT COMPANIES FOUNDATION
KITTY M. PERKINS FOUNDATION
LEU FOUNDATION, INC.
LINCOLN FOUNDATION, INC.
LLOYD A. FRY FOUNDATION
LOZIER FOUNDATION
MILTON S. & CORRINE N.
  LIVINGSTON FOUNDATION,
  INC.
MOODY FOUNDATION
NBC FOUNDATION, INC.
NORTHWEST AREA FOUNDATION
OMAHA COMMUNITY FOUNDATION
OMAHA WORLD-HERALD
  FOUNDATION

PAUL AND OSCAR GIGER
    FOUNDATION, INC.
PHELPS COUNTY COMMUNITY
    FOUNDATION, INC.
PHILADELPHIA FOUNDATION
PHILIP L. GRAHAM FUND
PINKERTON FOUNDATION
PITTSBURGH FOUNDATION
PEED FOUNDATION
QUIVEY-BAY STATE FOUNDATION
RANDOLPH FOUNDATION
RICHARD & RHONDA GOLDMAN
    FUND
ROBERT HERMAN STORZ
    FOUNDATION
ROBERT W. WOODRUFF
    FOUNDATION, INC.
ROGERS FOUNDATION
RON AND CAROL COPE
    FOUNDATION
ROY A. HUNT FOUNDATION
SAN FRANCISCO FOUNDATION
SHERMAN FAIRCHILD FOUNDATION
SHERWOOD FOUNDATION
SHUBERT FOUNDATION, INC.
SPENCER FOUNDATION
STEINHART FOUNDATION, INC.
STEWARDSHIP FOUNDATION
THOMAS D. BUCKLEY TRUST
VALMONT FOUNDATION
W.K. KELLOGG FOUNDATION
WELLER FOUNDATION
WIEBE CHARITABLE FOUNDATION
WOODS CHARITABLE FUND, INC.

ENDOWMENTS:

AMERICAN UNIVERSITY
THE ART INSTITUTE OF CHICAGO
BALL STATE UNIVERSITY
    FOUNDATION
BATES COLLEGE
BOSTON COLLEGE
BUCKNELL UNIVERSITY
BUENA VISTA COLLEGE

CANISIUS COLLEGE
CASE WESTERN RESERVE
    UNIVERSITY
CLARKSON UNIVERSITY
DARTMOUTH COLLEGE
DICKINSON COLLEGE
DRAKE UNIVERSITY
ELMHURST COLLEGE
HASTINGS COLLEGE
HENDRIX COLLEGE
HOFSTRA UNIVERSITY
INDIANA UNIVERSITY FOUNDATION
LEHIGH UNIVERSITY
LOMA LINDA UNIVERSITY
MERCER UNIVERSITY
MIAMI UNIVERSITY
NATIONAL GALLERY OF ART
NEBRASKA WESLEYAN UNIVERSITY
OREGON STATE UNIVERSITY
        FOUNDATION
PEDDIE SCHOOL
RADCLIFFE COLLEGE
REED COLLEGE
SOUTHERN METHODIST
    UNIVERSITY
ST. LAWRENCE UNIVERSITY
TEMPLE UNIVERSITY
TEXAS TECH UNIVERSITY
TUFTS UNIVERSITY
UNIVERSITY OF CHICAGO
UNIVERSITY OF ILLINOIS
UNIVERSITY OF IOWA FOUNDATION
UNIVERSITY OF MISSOURI SYSTEM
UNIVERSITY OF PENNSYLVANIA
UNIVERSITY OF PUGET SOUND
UNIVERSITY OF TEXAS SYSTEM
VANDERBILT UNIVERSITY
VASSAR COLLEGE
WASHINGTON UNIVERSITY
WASHINGTON & LEE UNIVERSITY
WASHINGTON STATE UNIVERSITY
WILLIAMS COLLEGE
YALE UNIVERSITY

Appendix D
LIST OF LARGE PUBLIC PENSION PLANS

R.S. OF ALABAMA

ALASKA DEPARTMENT OF REVENUE, TREASURY DIVISION

ALASKA PERMANENT FUND CORPORATION

ARIZONA STATE R.S.

ARKANSAS PUBLIC EMPLOYEES R.S.

ARKANSAS TEACHER R.S.

CALIFORNIA PUBLIC EMPLOYEES' R.S. (CalPERS)

CALIFORNIA STATE TEACHERS' R.S.

COLORADO PUBLIC EMPLOYEES' RETIREMENT ASSOCIATION

DENVER PUBLIC SCHOOL EMPLOYEES' PENSION & BENEFIT ASSOCIATION

STATE OF CONNECTICUT TRUST FUNDS

DELAWARE STATE EMPLOYEES RETIREMENT FUND

DISTRICT OF COLUMBIA RETIREMENT BOARD

FLORIDA STATE BOARD OF ADMINISTRATION

FLORIDA STATE TREASURY

GEORGIA PUBLIC EMPLOYEES' R.S.

GEORGIA TEACHERS R. S.

HAWAII EMPLOYEES' R.S.

IDAHO PUBLIC EMPLOYEE R.S.

CHICAGO MUNICIPAL EMPLOYEES' ANNUITY & BENEFIT FUND

PUBLIC SCHOOL TEACHERS' PENSION & RETIREMENT FUND OF CHICAGO

ILLINOIS MUNICIPAL RETIREMENT FUND

ILLINOIS TEACHERS' R.S.

INDIANA PUBLIC EMPLOYEES' RETIREMENT FUND

INDIANA STATE TEACHERS' RETIREMENT FUND

IOWA PUBLIC EMPLOYEES' R.S.

KANSAS PUBLIC EMPLOYEES' R. S.

KENTUCKY R.S.

KENTUCKY TEACHERS' R.S.

LOUISIANA STATE EMPLOYEES' R. S.

LOUISIANA TEACHERS' R.S.

MAINE STATE R.S.

MARYLAND STATE R.S.

MASSACHUSETTS PENSIONS RESERVE INVESTMENT MANAGEMENT BOARD

MASSACHUSETTS STATE TEACHERS' & EMPLOYEES' R.S.

MICHIGAN DEPARTMENT OF TREASURY

MINNESOTA STATE BOARD OF INVESTMENT

MISSISSIPPI PUBLIC EMPLOYEES' R. S.

MISSOURI STATE EMPLOYEES' R. S.

PUBLIC SCHOOL R. S. OF MISSOURI

MONTANA BOARD OF INVESTMENTS

NEVADA PUBLIC EMPLOYEES' R. S.

NEW HAMPSHIRE R.S.

NEW JERSEY DIVISION OF INVESTMENT

NEW MEXICO EDUCATIONAL RETIREMENT BOARD

NEW MEXICO PUBLIC EMPLOYEES' RETIREMENT ASSOCIATION

NEW MEXICO STATE PERMANENT FUND

NEW YORK CITY R.S.

NEW YORK STATE COMMON RETIREMENT FUND

NEW YORK STATE TEACHERS' R. S.

NORTH CAROLINA DEPARTMENT OF STATE TREASURER

NORTH DAKOTA PUBLIC EMPLOYEES' R.S.

OHIO POLICE & FIREMEN'S DISABILITY & PENSION BOARD

OHIO PUBLIC EMPLOYEES' R.S.

OHIO SCHOOL EMPLOYEES' R.S.

OHIO STATE TEACHERS' R.S.

OKLAHOMA PUBLIC EMPLOYEES'
   R.S.
OKLAHOMA TEACHERS' R.S.
OREGON PUBLIC EMPLOYEES' R. S.
PENNSYLVANIA PUBLIC SCHOOL
   EMPLOYEES' R. S.
PENNSYLVANIA STATE EMPLOYEES'
   R.S.
RHODE ISLAND R.S.
SOUTH CAROLINA R.S.
TENNESSEE CONSOLIDATED R.S.
TEXAS COUNTY AND DISTRICT R.S.

EMPLOYEES' R.S. OF TEXAS
TEXAS PERMANENT SCHOOL FUND
TEXAS MUNICIPAL R.S.
TEACHER R.S. OF TEXAS
UTAH STATE R.S.
VERMONT STATE R.S.
WASHINGTON STATE INVESTMENT
   BOARD
WEST VIRGINIA STATE BOARD OF
   INVESTMENTS
WISCONSIN INVESTMENT BOARD
WYOMING R.S.

Selected Bibliography

Admati, Anat R., Paul Pfleiderer, and Josef Zechner. "Large Shareholder Activism, Risk Sharing, and Financial Market Equilibrium." *Journal of Political Economy* 102, No. 6 (1994): 1097-1130.

Agrawal, Anup and Gershon N. Mandelker. "Large Shareholders and the Monitoring of Managers: the Case of Antitakeover Charter Amendments." *Journal of Financial and Quantitative Analysis* 25, No. 2 (1990): 143-166.

Alchian, Armen A. and Harold Demsetz. "Production, Information Costs, and Economic Organization." *The American Economic Journal* 62 (1972): 777-795.

Armstrong, J. Scott and Terry S. Overton. "Estimating Nonresponse Bias in Mail Surveys." *Journal of Marketing Research* 16 (1977): 396-402.

Ayers, Ian and Peter Cramton. "Relational Investing and Agency Theory." *Cardozo Law Review* 15 (1994): 1033-1066.

Bainbridge, Stephen M. "The Politics of Corporate Governance." *Harvard Journal of Law & Public Policy* 18, No. 3 (1995): 671-734.

Barclay, Michael J. and Clifford G. Holderness. "Private Benefits from Control of Public Corporations." *Journal of Financial Economics* 25 (1989): 371-395.

Barnard, Chester. *The Function of the Executive*. Cambridge, MA: Harvard University Press, 1938.

Barnard, Jayne W. "Institutional Investors and the New Corporate Governance." *North Carolina Law Review* 69 (1991): 1135-1187.

Bateman, Brenda O. *How Institutions Voted on Social Policy Shareholder Resolutions in the 1993 Proxy Season*. Washington, D.C.: Investor Responsibility Research Center, Inc., 1993.

Baum, Daniel J. and Ned B. Stiles. *The Silent Partners: Institutional Investors and Corporate Control.* Syracuse, NY: Syracuse University Press, 1965.

Berle, Adolph A. and Gardiner C. Means. *The Modern Corporation and Private Property.* New York: Macmillan, 1932.

Black, Bernard S. "Agents Watching Agents: The Promise of Institutional Investor Voice." *UCLA Law Review* 39 (1992): 811-893.

_____. "The Value of Institutional Investor Monitoring: the Empirical Evidence." *UCLA Law Review* 39 (1992): 895-939.

_____ and John C. Coffee, Jr. "Hail Britannia?: Institutional Investor Behavior under Limited Regulation." *Michigan Law Review* 92, No. 7 (1994): 1997-2087.

Blair, Margaret M. *Ownership and Control: Rethinking Corporate Governance for the Twenty-first Century.* Washington, DC: The Brookings Institution, 1995.

_____. *Wealth Creation and Wealth Sharing: A Colloquium on Corporate Governance and Investments in Human Capital.* Washington, DC: The Brookings Institution, 1996.

Boyd, Brian K. "Ceo Duality and Firm Performance: A Contingency Model." *Strategic Management Journal* 16 (1995): 301-312.

Brickley, James A., Ronald C. Lease, and Clifford W. Smith, Jr. "Ownership Structure and Voting on Antitakeover Amendments." *Journal of Financial Economics* 20 (1988): 267-291.

CalSTERS. 1996 *Annual Comprehensive Financial Report of the California State Teachers' Retirement System.* Sacramento, Ca: CalSTERS, 1996.

Carleton, Willard T., James M. Nelson, and Michael S. Weisbach. "The Influence of Institutions on Corporate Governance Through Private Negotiations: Evidence from TIAA-CREF." *Journal of Finance* 53, No. 4 (1998): 1335-1362.

Carter, Nancy M., Timothy M. Stearns, Paul D. Reynolds, and Brenda A. Miller. "New Venture Strategies: Theory Development with an Empirical Base." *Strategic Management Journal* 15, No. 1 (1994): 21-41.

Chaganti, Rajeswararao and Fariborz Damanpour. "Institutional Ownership, Capital Structure and Firm Performance." *Strategic Management Journal* 12 (1991): 479-491.

Coffee, John C., Jr. "The SEC and the Institutional Investor: a Half-time Report." *Cardozo Law Review* 15 (1994): 837-907.

Conard, Alfred F. "Beyond Managerialism: Investor Capitalism." *Journal of Law Reform* 22, No. 1 (1988): 117-178.

Corporate Governance Advisor. *Big Problems at Small Companies for CalPERS* 4, No. 2 (March/April 1996): 29.

Crowell, Richard A. and Robert E. Mainer. "Pension Fund Management: External or Internal?" *Harvard Business Review.* 58, No. 6(1980): 180-182.

Daily, Catherine M., Jonathon L. Johnson, Alan E. Ellstrand, and Dan R. Dalton. *Institutional Investor Activism: Follow the Leaders?* Paper Presented at Annual Meeting of the Academy of Management, Boston, Massachusetts, 9-14 August 1996.

Davis, Gerald F. and Tracy A. Thompson. "A Social Movement Perspective on Corporate Control." *Administrative Science Quarterly* 39 (1994): 141-173.

Davis, James H., F. David Schoorman, and Lax Donaldson. "Towards a Stewardship Theory of Management." *Academy of Management Review* 22 (1997): 20–47.

Del Guercio, Diane and Jennifer Hawkins. *The Motivation and Impact of Pension Fund Activism.* Working Paper, University of Oregon, 1997.

Demsetz, Harold. "The Structure of Ownership and the Theory of the Firm." *Journal of Law and Economics* 26 (1983): 375-390.

_____ and Kenneth Lehn. "The Structure of Ownership: Causes and Consequences." *Journal of Political Economy* 93 (1983): 1155-1177.

Dill, William R. "Public Participation in Corporate Planning: Strategic Management in a Kibitzer's World." *Long Range Planning* 8, No. 1 (1975): 57-63.

Dobrzynski, Judith H. "Relationship Investing: A New Shareholder Is Emerging - Patient and Involved." *Business Week* 15 March 1993, 68-75.

Dodds, E. Merrick, Jr. "For Whom Are Corporate Managers Trustees?" *Harvard Law Review* 45, No. 7 (1932): 1145-1163.

DOL, "Interpretive Bulletin Relating to Written Statements of Investment Policy, Including Proxy Voting Policy and Guidelines." *Code of Federal Regulations* 29, Sec. 2509.94-2. Washington, DC: National Archives and Records Administration, 1 July 1998.

Donaldson, Lex. "The Ethereal Hand: Organizational Economics and Management Theory." *Academy of Management Review* 15 (1990): 369-381.

_____. "A Rational Basis for Criticisms of Organizational Economics: A Reply to Barney." *Academy of Management Review* 15 (1990): 394-401.

_____ and J. H. Davis. "Stewardship Theory or Agency Theory: CEO Governance and Shareholder Returns." *Australian Journal of Management* 16 (1991): 49-64.

Eakins, Stan. "An Empirical Investigation of Monitoring by Institutional Investors." *American Business Review* (January 1995): 67-74.

Fama, Eugene F. and Michael C. Jensen. "Separation of Ownership and Control." *Journal of Law & Economics* 26 (1983): 301-325.

Fisch, Jill E. "Relationship Investing: Will it Happen? Will it Work?" *Ohio State Law Journal* 55, No. 5 (1994): 1009-1048.

Foundation Center. *The Foundation Directory: 1996 Edition.* New York: The Foundation Center, 1996.

Fowler, Floyd J., Jr. *Improving Survey Questions: Design and Evaluation.* Thousand Oaks, CA: Sage Publications, 1995.

Fox, Mark A. and Robert T. Hamilton. "Ownership and Diversification: Agency Theory or Stewardship Theory." *Journal of Management Studies* 31, No. 1 (1994): 69-81.

Garten, Helen. "Institutional Investors and the New Financial Order." *Rutgers Law Review* 44 (1992): 585-674.

Gerber, Susan B. and Kristin E. Voelkl. *The SPSS Guide to the New Statistical Analysis of Data.* New York: Springer-Verlag New York Inc., 1997.

Ghoshal, Sumantra and Peter Moran. "Bad for Practice: a Critique of the Transaction Cost Theory." *Academy of Management Review* 21 (1996): 13-57.

Gilson, Ronald J. *Corporate Governance and Economic Efficiency: When Do Institutions Matter?* Working Paper No. 121, Stanford University Law School, 1996, 1-31.

_____. And Reinier Kraakman. "Reinventing the Outside Director: An Agenda for Institutional Investors." *Stanford Law Review* 43 (1991): 863-906.

_____. And _____. "Institutional Investors, Portfolio Performance and Corporate Governance." Ed. A. Sametz. *Institutional Investing: The Challenges and Responsibilities of the Twenty-first Century.* Homewood, IL: Business One Irwin, 1991.

Glasberg, Davita S. and Michael Schwartz. "Ownership and Control of Corporations." *Annual Review of Sociology* 9 (1983): 311-332.

Gordon, Jeffrey N. "Institutions as Relational Investors: A New Look at Cumulative Voting." *Columbia Law Review* 94 (1994): 124-198.

Gordon, Lilli A. and John Pound. "Information, Ownership Structure, and Shareholder Voting: Evidence from Shareholder-sponsored Corporate Governance Proposals. *Journal of Finance* 48 (1993): 697-718.

_____ and _____. *Active Investing in the U.S. Equity Market: Past Performance and Future Prospects.* Monograph. Gordon Group, Inc., 1993.

Gough, Newell. *Institutional Activists at Poorly Performing Firms: Do They Make a Difference in the Turnaround?* Paper Presented at the 15th Annual International Conference of the Strategic Management Society. Mexico City, 1995.

Graves, Samuel B. and Sandra A. Waddock. "Institutional Ownership and Control: Implications for Long-term Corporate Strategy." *Academy of Management Executive* 4, No. 1 (1990): 75-83.

Grundfest, Joseph A. "Subordination of American Capital." *Journal of Financial Economics* 27 (1990): 89-114.

Harrison, Jeffrey S. and Caron H. St. John, "Managing and Partnering with External Stakeholders," *Academy of Management Executive* 10, No. 2 (1996): 46-60.

Hawley, James P. and Andrew T. Williams. "The Emergence of Fiduciary Capitalism." *Corporate Governance* 5, No. 4 (1997): 206-213.

_____ and _____. "Corporate Governance in the United States: The Rise of Fiduciary Capitalism: A Review of the Literature," [paper on-line] (Portland, Me.: Lens, Inc., 1996); available from http://www.lens-inc.com/info/papers96/first/firstcontents.htm; Internet; accessed 26 January 1999.

_____, _____, and John U. Miller. "Getting the Herd to Run: Shareholder Activism at the California Public Employees' Retirement System (CalPERS)." *Business & the Contemporary World* 7, no. 4 (1994): 26-48.

Hill, Charles W.L.and Scott A.Snell. "External Control, Corporate Strategy, and Firm Performance in Research-intensive Industries." *Strategic Management Journal* 9 (1988): 577-590.

Hirschman, Albert O. Exit, *Voice and Loyalty: Responses to Decline in Firms, Organizations and States.* Cambridge, MA: Harvard University Press. 1970.

Holl, Peter. "The Effect of Control Type on the Performance of the Firm in the U.K." *The Journal of Industrial Economics* 23, No. 4 (1975): 257-271.

Hoskisson, Robert E., Michael A. Hitt, Richard A. Johnson, and Wayne Grossman. Conflicting Voices: the Effects of Ownership Heterogeneity and Internal Governance on Corporate Strategy. Paper Presented at Annual Meeting of the Academy of Management, Boston, Massachusetts, 9-14 August 1996.

Investor Responsibility Research Center. *Corporate Governance Service: Voting Results 1993.* Washington, DC: Investor Responsibility Research Center, 1994. 1-47.

Jensen, Michael C. "The Modern Industrial Revolution, Exit and the Failure of Internal Control Systems." *Journal of Finance* 43, No. 3 (1993): 831-880.

_____ and William H. Meckling. "Theory of the Firm: Managerial Behavior, Agency Costs and Ownership Structure." *Journal of Financial Economics* 3 (1976): 305–360.

Kamerschen, David R. "The Influence of Ownership and Control on Profit Rates." *The American Economic Review* 58 (1968): 432-447.

Karpoff, Jonathan M., Paul H. Malatesta, and Ralph A. Walking. *Corporate Governance and Shareholder Initiatives: Empirical Evidence.* Working Paper, Ohio State University, 1996, 1- 36.

Kensinger, John W. and John D. Martin. *Relationship Investing: What Active Institutional Investors Want from Management.* Morristown, NJ: Financial Executives Research Foundation, Inc, 1996.

Kleiman, Robert T., Kevin Nathan, and Joel M. Shulman. "Are There Payoffs for "Patient" Corporate Investors?" *Mergers & Acquisitions* (March/April 1994): 34-41.

Kochhar, Rahul & Parthiban David. "Institutional Investors and Firm Innovation: a Test of Competing Hypotheses." *Strategic Management Journal* 17, No 1 (1996): 73-84.

Koppes, Richard H. and Maureen L. Reilly. "An Ounce of Prevention: Meeting the Fiduciary Duty to Monitor an Index Fund Through Relationship Investing." *The Journal of Corporation Law* 20, No. 3 (1995): 413-449.

Kumar, Nirmalya, Louis W. Stern, and James C. Anderson. "Conducting Interorganizational Research Using Key Informants." *Academy of Management Journal* 36 (1993): 1633-1651.

Lashbrooke, E.C., Jr. "The Divergence of Corporate Finance and Law in Corporate Governance." *South Carolina Law Review* 46 (1995): 449-469.

Lipton, Martin, Theodore N. Mirvis, and Steven A. Rosenblum. "Corporate Governance in the Era of Institutional Ownership." *New York University Law Review* 70 (1995): 1145-1166.

Lublin, Joann S. "Unions Brandish Stock to Force Change." *The Wall Street Journal*, 17 May 1996, B1,B6.

Matheson, John H. and Brent A. Olson. "Corporate Cooperation, Relationship Management and the Trialogical Imperative for Corporate Law." *Minnesota Law Review*. 78 (1994): 1443–1491.

McConnell, John J. and Henri Servaes. "Additional Evidence on Equity Ownership and Corporate Value." *Journal of Financial Economics* 27 (1990): 595–612.

McConville, Daniel J. "Plan Management." *Pension Management* 31, No. 8 (1995): 6-7.

McEachern, William A. *Managerial Control and Performance.* Lexington, MA: D.C. Heath and Company, 1975.

McGee, Jeffrey E. and Michael J. "Responding to Increased Environmental Hostility: A Study of the Competitive Behavior of Small Retailers." *Journal of Applied Business Research* 13, No. 1 (1996): 83-94.

Miles, Morgan P. and Danny R. Arnold. "The Relationship Between Marketing Orientation and Entrepreneurial Orientation." *Entrepreneurship Theory and Practice* 15, No. 4 (1991): 49-65.

Milgrom, Paul and John Roberts. *Economics, Organization and Management.* Englewood Cliffs, NJ: Prentice Hall, 1992.

Millstein, Ira M. and Lee Smith. *Our Money's Worth: The Report of the Governor's Task Force on Pension Fund Investment.* New York: New York State Industrial Cooperation Council, 1992.

Minnesota State Board of Investment. *The 1996 Annual Report of the Minnesota State Board of Investment*. St. Paul, MN: Minnesota State Board of Investment, 1996.

Money Market. *The Directory of Pension Funds and Their Investment Managers*. 25th Ed. Charlottesville, VA: The Money Market Directories, Inc, 1995.

Monsen, R. Joseph, John S. Chiu, and David E. Cooley. "The Effect of Separation of Ownership and Control on the Performance of the Large Firm." *Quarterly Journal of Economics* 82 (1968): 435-451.

Morck, Randall, Andrei Shleifer, and Robert W. Vishny. "Management Ownership and Market Valuation: An Empirical Analysis." *Journal of Financial Economics* 20 (1988): 293-315.

Nesbitt, Stephen L. "Long-term Rewards from Shareholder Activism: A Study of the 'CalPERS Effect.'" *Journal of Applied Corporate Finance* (Winter 1994): 75–80.

O'Barr, William M. and John M. Conley. *Fortune and Folly: The Wealth and Power of Institutional Investing*. Homewood, IL: Business One Irwin, 1992.

Opler, Tim C. and Jonathon Sokobin. *Does Coordinated Institutional Activism Work? An Analysis of the Activities of the Council of Institutional Investors*. Working Paper, Ohio State University, 1995, 1–26.

Palmiter, Alan R. "The Shareholder Proposal Rule: A Failed Experiment in Merit Regulation." *Alabama Law Review* 45 (1994): 879-926.

Podsakoff, Philip M. and Dennis W. Organ. "Self-reports in Organizational Research: Problems and Prospects." *Journal of Management* 12, No. 4 (1986): 531–544.

Porter, Michael E. *Capital Choices: Changing the Way America Invests in Industry*. Washington, DC: Research Report Presented by the Council on Competitiveness and Cosponsored by the Harvard Business School, 1992.

Pound, John. "The Rise of the Political Model of Corporate Governance and Corporate Control." *New York University Law Review* 68 (1993): 1003–1071.

Pozen, Robert C. "Institutional Investors: The Reluctant Activists." *Harvard Business Review* 1994: 140-149.

Radice, H. K. "Control Type, Profitability and Growth in Large Firms: An Empirical Study." *The Economic Journal* 81 (1971): 547–562.

Rock, Edward B. "The Logic and (Uncertain) Significance of Institutional Shareholder Activism." *The Georgetown Law Journal* 79 (1991): 445-506.

Roe, Mark J. *Strong Managers, Weak Owners: The Political Roots of American Corporate Finance*. Princeton, NJ: Princeton University Press, 1994.

Romano, Roberta. "Public Pension Fund Activism in Corporate Governance Reconsidered." *Columbia Law Review* 94 (1993): 795-853.

Russell Reynolds Associates. *Redefining Corporate Governance: 1995 U.S. Survey of Institutional Investors.* New York: Russell Reynolds Associates, 1995.

Schlossberger, Eugene. "A New Model of Business: Dual-investor Theory." *Business Ethics Quarterly* 4, No. 4 (1994): 459–474.

Schultz, Ellen E. and Susan Warren. "Pension System Ousts Company's Board in Big Victory for Institutional Investors." *The Wall Street Journal*, 29 May 1998: A2.

Schwab, Stewart J and Randall S. Thomas. "Realigning Corporate Governance: Shareholder Activism by Labor Unions." *Michigan Law Review* 96, No. 4 (1998): 1018-1094.

Sherman, Hugh, Sam Beldona, and Maheshkumar P. Joshi. *Institutional Investors: Four Distinctive Types.* Paper Presented at Annual Meeting of the Southern Management Association, New Orleans, Louisiana, 5–10 November 1996.

Shleifer, Andrei and Robert W. Vishny. "Large Shareholders and Corporate Control." *Journal of Political Economy* 94 (1986): 461–488.

_____ and _____. "A Survey of Corporate Governance." *The Journal of Finance* 52, no. 2 (1997): 737–783.

Shortell, Stephen M. and Edward J. Zajac. "Perceptual and Archival Measures of Miles and Snow's Strategic Types: A Comprehensive Assessment of Reliability and Validity." *Academy of Management Journal* 33 (1990): 817-832.

Smith, Adam. *An Inquiry into the Nature and Causes of the Wealth of Nations.* New York: E.P. Dutton & Co, 1931.

Smith, Michael P. "Shareholder Activism by Institutional Investors: Evidence from CalPERS." *The Journal of Finance* 51 (1996): 227–252

Steer, Peter and John Cable. "Internal Organization and Profit: An Empirical Analysis of Large U.K. Companies." *The Journal of Industrial Economics* 27, No. 1 (1975): 13–30.

Strickland, Deon, Kenneth W. Wiles, and Marc W. Zenner. "A Requiem for the USA: Is Small Shareholder Monitoring Effective?" *Journal of Financial Economics* 40 (1996): 319–338.

Taylor, William. "Can Big Owners Make a Big Difference?" *Harvard Business Review* 68, No. 5 (1990): 70–82.

Turnbull, Shaun. "Corporate Governance: Its Scope, Concerns and Theories." *Corporate Governance* 5, No 4 (1997): 180–205.

Useem, Michael. *Investor Capitalism: How Money Managers Are Changing the Face of Corporate America.* New York: Basic Books, 1996.

Wahal, Sunil. "Pension Fund Activism and Firm Performance." *Journal of Financial & Quantitative Analysis* 31, No 1 (1996): 1–23.

Weiss Rating. *Weiss' Ratings Insurance Safety Directory.* Palm Beach Gardens, FL: Weiss Publication, Inc, 1996.

Wright, Peter, Stephen P. Ferris, Atulya Sarin, and Vidya Awasthi. "Impact of Corporate Insider, Blockholder, and Institutional Equity Ownership on Firm Risk Taking." *Academy of Management Journal* 39(1996): 441-463.

Zeckhauser, Richard J. & John Pound. "Are Large Shareholders Effective Monitors? An Investigation of Share Ownership and Corporate Performance" Ed. R. Glenn Hubbard, *Asymmetric Information, Corporate Finance and Investment*. Chicago, IL: The University of Chicago Press. 6 (1990): 149–180.

Index

*For Product Safety Concerns and Information please contact
our EU representative GPSR@taylorandfrancis.com Taylor & Francis
Verlag GmbH, Kaufingerstraße 24, 80331 München, Germany*

T - #0053 - 160425 - C0 - 216/138/11 [13] - CB - 9780815335023 - Gloss Lamination